The Trail to
The Iditarod Trail

By Jackai Szuhai
© 2003JSz

Published by
Dynagraphix Desktop Publishing
Schofield, WI
2003

The Trail to the Iditarod Trail

Second Edition

Acknowledgements

This book would never have come into existence without some serious help from a lot of people.

First and foremost of course are Betty and David Britz and the entire Eskimo Bandit Kennel, without whom the whole trip would never have happened. Also special thanks to them for trusting me to come back to the lower 48 and tell their story.

Second are the friends and family who looked after my own place and critters so I had the freedom to take such a trip.

*Lori Ross and Robin Graham who worked hard at my house to make sure the needs of all the animals were met. They were there to deliver Lily's litter when I couldn't be. They even made sure that Zsa Zsa got down to Laural for the shows so she could finish her AKC championship.

*Kay Ross and Chris Ross who were Lori and Robin's backup team.

*Delores Lieske who was there for Lori and my little Lily. Also she is the photographer for most of the really good pictures in this book!

Certainly no less important are the many friends and volunteers who helped with the actual creation and production of this book.

* Rebecca Montee who encouraged me from the start and who guided me through rough spots. Help with editing and organization and getting many photos in the form necessary to get included in this book were only part of her contribution.

*Sharon Solheim and Joe Regester from LakesArea dot com who helped immensely with planning, pictures and publicity.

*Jane and Vern Elliott of Dynagraphix Desktop Publishing and Arctic Air Development, respectively, who did the actual final edits, formatting, layout and publishing... absolutely priceless help from priceless people.

* Drenda and Joe Vijuk for their generosity in the original printing of the first edition of this book.

*And many other people who contributed in so many ways it would be absolutely impossible to name them all.

****and...Mom!

The Trail to the Iditarod Trail

Preface

Most of this book is a journal of the trip to Alaska on which I was fortunate enough to accompany the All Alaskan Malamute Iditarod Dream Team.

Much of it follows the day to day notes we kept. There are a few places where I inserted information that I acquired after returning from the journey. When I did this I tried to set it off by italicizing the print. The exceptions to this are the chapters I wrote on the races after returning to the lower 48 and researching backgrounds, and of course the epilogue.

The astute reader may notice changes in tense. Sometimes I seem to hop from present to past and back again. This is intentional because that is the way I recorded it. Some of it was recorded with the feeling that it was happening then. I frequently write in my head and actually put it down on paper when I have the chance. Some of it was written in the evening looking back at the day.

I only hope that in this book I convey to you, the reader, some of the positive strength, care and devotion that the people I have written about live as their everyday lives.

The Couple

The tall slender young woman moved gracefully through the pet shop. The mass of dark curls surrounding her innocent- looking face disappeared into the background when she raised her large brown eyes. When she spoke, her soft almost childlike voice could command the attention of virtually any man with a pulse. The shop owner rushed to give his attention to this attractive potential customer. Much to his surprise she was not there to shop. Instead she berated him for selling puppies and for the conditions in which they were kept. A serious discussion ensued. The shop owner was not a bad person. He was surprised to find that the puppies he carried as merchandise actually came from puppy mills. When he bought them from the puppy broker he believed that the puppies had been purchased from responsible breeders. He didn't know that responsible breeders would have nothing to do with puppy brokers.

As the dark eyed beauty educated him, the two of them were observed by a tall blond man. His blue eyes sometimes narrowed and sometimes sparkled as he watched the animated conversation.

The final outcome of the discussion was that the shop owner hired the young woman to improve conditions in the shop for the animals and to generally make the shop more highly reputable.

The next day as she began working to improve the shop, she noticed that the tall man with the chiseled Nordic features had returned. He continued to return on a daily basis. Eventually they developed a firm and lasting friendship. This was later to grow into a strong and lifelong love.

If someone were writing a fiction novel, it would certainly make no sense for a couple like this to meet at a pet shop in the biggest shopping mall in Green Bay, Wisconsin. I guess truth really is stranger than fiction.

Betty Welles was there because that was her hometown. She had discovered her love of animals as a student in St. Joseph grade school years before. By the fifth grade she was working in the pet animal laboratory. While she attended South West High School she took college level courses offered to accelerated science students. She worked with small and large animal veterinary and parasite control courses. For her excellent performance she earned a work-study program with the Green Bay Animal Hospital and Pet Clinic. When she graduated from South West HS in 1979 she received a full scholarship to the University of Minnesota to work in the field of veterinary medicine.

While she was studying to become a veterinarian, Betty began to have very serious issues with her health. She became very ill with low blood sugar problems. She has had diabetes since she was five years old. She wasn't diagnosed until she was six years old, when her parents took her to the hospital in a coma. Although it had been under control for years, while she was at the university it suddenly flared up and took a more serious turn. Her condition was discussed among the staff and she was informed that because of the brittle state of her health, she would never be able to practice veterinary medicine. This was a huge disappointment to Betty.

To this day she must deal with the problems and challenges of her diabetes. With the advent of the insulin pump, she has made some progress but she still has to be very careful and aware of her chemical balances day to day, often hour to hour.

Although her hopes were crushed in one area, she would not, could not forsake her love of animals. Besides taking the job in the pet shop, which she turned into high quality pet supply store, she became interested in dog training. She joined Packerland Dog Training School and continued to take

2

courses in dog training for many years, there and elsewhere. She trained her first malamute in obedience and conformation showing and became involved in working dog activities such as weight-pulling, dogsledding and skijouring. The more she

does, the more she wants to do.

Betty calls her dogs her fur children. She says they are her lifeline. With them she reaches out to people of all ages. She teaches about dogs and other animals, about training, obedience, conformation, working, basic care, grooming and animal behavior. She also reaches out to touch people and encourage them to love animals and each other.

The journey of David Britz to that fateful day in the pet shop in Green Bay started longer ago and further away, when he was born in Trenton, a suburb of Detroit, MI. His whole family moved to Houghton, in Michigan's Upper Peninsula, when he was just two years old. He remained there until he graduated from Houghton High School. From there he went to St. Louis, Missouri, for training in diesel mechanics and graduated from Bailey Tech. in 1970. He volunteered to serve his country in Vietnam and was there for nearly three years. He came home to a bitter America.

He returned to school at the Michigan Institute of Technology and became a certified welder in 1979, and a graduate of Machine Tool in 1980.

He also grew up loving dogs. It was just a natural part of his makeup. By the time he was nine years old he was running his first dog team. With no real teacher for it, he had cut up old blue jeans to make harnesses and trained his pet dogs to run and pull. He didn't get his first Siberian Husky until 1977. He enjoyed going to dogsled races in the area to watch and help out.

David moved to Green Bay for a job. Browsing in the Mall in his spare time one day, he happened upon a pet shop and went in to look at the puppies. There he discovered a beautiful young woman with morals, ethics and principles and the courage to speak up for them He listened to the animated exchange between her and the shop owner at first with amusement and then with admiration.

The following day he returned to the shop on the chance that she might be there. She was. When he found out that she had taken a job there, he dropped in on a daily basis.

They struck up a conversation. At that time Betty was dating another man, but they were too much alike to allow this opportunity to escape entirely. Perhaps they knew deep down there was something special here not to be missed.

They became friends. They talked about animals, dogs especially. Each learned how much the other loved animals. Each of them also learned of the others' interest in sled dogs. Before long they were going with each other to dog related activities in the area. They especially liked to go to the dogsled races.

At that time David owned one Siberian husky. Betty owned her first three malamutes. David was fascinated by the dogsled racing. Betty encouraged him. Pretty soon David had a team of Siberians and was running sprint races. Betty also ran the sprints with her three malamute team and weight-pulled them as well.

David added Alaskan huskies to his team. Betty encouraged him and often bought dogs for him. She was happy with her malamutes but if he enjoyed other dogs that was fine with

4

her. She has always loved all kinds of dogs.

One day Betty found out that she had been betrayed by her boyfriend. She has always been such an honest, sincere person that she could never understand that others are not always like that. She was deeply hurt.

Of course her loyal friend David consoled her. He allowed her to spill out her grief. He was angry with that fool for hurting her but deep down he was probably glad to see him gone. David remained Betty's steadfast friend.

(Well, dear readers, I know we can all see this coming.)

Of course the next thing to do was the most natural of all. The two them fell deeply and permanently in love....and there they stay to this very day.

They were married in 1985.

In 1986 David needed to return to Houghton, MI, to take care of his ailing mother, so they took themselves and all their dogs and moved north.

Before long Betty's malamutes had also won David's heart. He found that he thoroughly enjoyed running them on the trails too. At that time freight races were a way of leveling the field for the bigger dogs to enjoy racing also. One hundred pounds of weight per dog was added to the sled of each team in a freight race.

In 1989 the Eskimo Bandit team won their first United States Freight Race Championship! They won every annual United States Freight Race Championship after that, from then through 1995. ISDRA has not run Freight Race Championships since then. That leaves them as the standing Freight Race champions. They have also been declared the Best All Alaskan Malamute Freight Team by ISDRA (the International Sled Dog Racing Association).

 From 1993 through 1995 they also ran the Mid-distance races. Mid-distance races are those equaling 200 miles or more. With David driving the Alaskan malamute team, they finished every race they entered, and they never placed last. When they tell people about it they are not including the team's that didn't finish at all. They only include all of the teams to finish. Ever since then, they have weight-pulled with their dogs and done many educational events and demonstrations.

Throughout their life together, they have also done animal rescue. Working with other official rescue organizations but usually working on their own, the Britz family has rescued many unwanted and often abused animals. They have gotten them necessary medical treatment and spent untold hours working and training and then finding just the right new home for several dozen innocent creatures, mostly canine but many others too. All of this has been done and paid for out of their own pockets.

Though they have sold most of the puppies from litters that they have bred (those that they didn't keep themselves) to wonderful loving homes, the Britz's have had a few very serious disappointments. They have always felt a lifelong obligation to all of their puppies to be sure they are in proper situations. Because the right placement and complete follow-up are so time consuming, Betty and David do not breed very many litters. Though they have been approached several times by racers who requested to use the Britz dogs at stud to improve the feet on some of their Alaskan huskies, they have always refused. (In fact they recently refused to sell a puppy to someone who wanted him for that purpose). They love all dogs. They know, however, of all the dogs literally dying for lack of good homes. The only breeding they do is to try to preserve the utmost quality in the breed they love so much.

Throughout their life in Michigan they have both been involved in serving their community. They have done social care and educational programs for young people, adults and senior citizens. David was a member of the volunteer fire department from the 1980's right up to the time they left for Alaska. He has been a member of the Reserves for years. He has just changed his home base to Ft. Richardson, Anchorage, Alaska.

Author's note: Most of the quotes and a definite majority of the information in this book come directly from Betty. There are two reasons for this.
(1) Betty is the one who has actually put pen to paper with much of the information contained herein.
(2) Betty is usually the one speaking to me when I am within reach of a pencil and paper.
It is important to realize that David is just as enthusiastic and as caring of all of these dogs as well as the whole adventure... However if the readers out there choose to give David the romantic image of the "strong, silent type" ... well... ok...

●   ●   ●   ●   ●   ●

For the purposes of the coming story, you'll need to know about the other two people on this trip. I will try to keep it brief.

Douglas I. Johnson was born December 22, 1920 in Atlantic Mine, MI, a suburb of Houghton, MI. He spent his childhood there, attended Atlantic Mine Elementary School and graduated from high school in 1936. He stayed in the area and worked, first at a gas station and then as a truck driver. In 1938 he worked for the Copper Range Railroad. In 1940 he was working for the Isle Royale Copper Mine as a ranger on Isle Royale.

In 1942 Douglas received greetings from the president of the United States. He left Atlantic Mine, MI and became a member of the First Cavalry. With them he went to Australia, New Guinea, Oro Bay, and Manila. They freed 3,700 prisoners of war, and then went on to Yokohama, and Tokyo, Japan. Douglas left Japan in 1945 on the USS General Pope, and arrived back in the USA at San Francisco. He was transferred to Camp McCoy, WI where he received his discharge on October 22, 1945. He had served two years, four months and five days. He was proud to serve his country and very happy to be back home again.

He returned to Atlantic Mine where he got work, first dry cleaning, then with the Houghton County Road Commission. He drove and maintained snow plows and trucks, sometimes working as long as 90 hours per week. He kept that job for 35 years and retired from the county in 1983.

In 1957 he traveled to Milwaukee, Wisconsin, where he attended technical school and learned about generators, alternators and starters. He opened his own business, **Doug's Auto Electric**, which he maintained until 1992 and then only worked part-time until he departed on this trip to Alaska.

Doug met his wife, Ann, in the nearby town of Hancock, Michigan in 1962. They married in June of 1963 and had fifteen happy years. In 1978 Ann had a stroke and became paralyzed on her right side. Doug took care of her for nineteen years at home, until his own failing health made that impossible. Ann was moved to the Houghton Medical Care facility where she remains now.

Doug's own health had deteriorated to the point that he needed some care and assistance to remain in his own home. One of the things that Betty did in service to their community that didn't have to do with the dogs, was to help care for older citizens. Doug became one of them. Soon Doug, Betty and David became fast friends. As Doug's condition gradually improved, he enjoyed acquiring the little Welsh spitfire with the golden coat who he calls Dehlia.

When David and Betty decided to go to Alaska, he persuaded them to take him along. In doing so Douglas left the home that he had built for himself and lived in for years. It was within 100 yards of the spot where he was born. Nevertheless, he was anxious and enthusiastic to go.

•   •   •   •   •   •

The fourth member of this traveling party, is the author of this book. She was born in Wisconsin where she attended school and college and graduated some years ago. When a four-year-old dogsledding companion of hers was asked "How old is Jackai?" She very seriously replied,"Older than dirt". The author chooses to leave it at that.

This person has taught every level of basic public school and some post-high school courses. She spent 30 active years in the sport of judo, of which she still employs the theories and principles to everyday life and very much to animal handling and training. She has loved animals, especially dogs and horses, all of her life, much to the distress and boredom of most of her family and many of her acquaintances. She spent several years working horses professionally. Riding horses of various breeds and structures along with the years of studying the mechanics and efficiency of movement (in Judo) have been of infinite value in her quest for excellent and correct movement and power in what she considers the ultimate of all working dogs, the Alaskan Malamute.

She has been a dog trainer since she was a teenager. (According to the same youngster that gave her age above, her first lead the dog was a brontosaurus.)

One valuable piece of advice this author might offer readers is,"Don't say something you don't mean."

In light of a conversation or two that went something like ....

"Well, if there's anything I can do for you...."
"You know we're leaving soon for Alaska."
"Well, if I can be of any help....."

"Maybe there's something you can do."

"Well of course, I don't have much money, so I can't be any real help there..... but if there's anything I can actually do..."

"There might be something."

"I'd sure like to help but I'm not very strong or mechanically inclined. About all I can do is read, write, and drive."

"....you like to drive?"

"Yes, I enjoy driving. I can drive just about anything."

"We were supposed to get another truck. We need it for all of our equipment... then we would need somebody to drive it."

"Oh...well...   too bad you didn't get it. I would have driven it for you."

"Really ?"

"Oh sure.... too bad you don't have it"

"Let me call you back... I'll make a few calls...... I'll talk to you later."

"Uh...ok"

Actually, what she really might advise would be to enjoy every opportunity because you might pass up the adventure of a lifetime, and that would be a real shame. In the words of a movie character, *"Life's a banquet... and most poor suckers are starving."*

Anyone who knows me, knows I'm not starving!

•   •   •   •   •   •

Another individual needs to be mentioned. He was not a member of this traveling party, but he was a very real factor in the encouragement and enthusiasm for the whole venture.

Colonel Norman D. Vaughan, a member of the first Byrd Antarctic Expedition 1928-1930, was the first American to drive dogs in the Antarctic. He was the chief dog driver for the Geological Party, and for his contributions Admiral Byrd named a mountain in his honor. On December 16, 1994, three days before his 89th birthday, Norman Vaughan reached the summit of Mount Vaughan, 10,302', in the Antarctic.

His background includes but is not necessarily limited to: Byrd Antarctic Expedition 1928-1930. Winter Olympics 1932. World War II Air Force Search and Rescue with 425 dogs: Instigated rescue of 24 air crew, 1942 Greenland, and single-handedly recovered Norden bomb site off B-17; Took 209 sled dogs to the Battle of the Bulge. First lower 48 team to compete in North American Championship, 1952. Presidential parades, 1973, 1977, 1981. Gave Pope John II dogsled ride, 1981. Entered Thirteen Iditarods, latest finish 1990 at age 84. Musher awards: Most Inspirational Musher, 1987; Timberland Spirit of the Iditarod Award, 1989; Musher of the Year, 1990; Musher Hall of Fame, 1990.

Author's note: The above information was copied directly from a commemorative business card which was given to David by Norman Vaughan himself, the first time the two of them met. It is an incredibly condensed version, even perhaps rather modest, of an incredible lifelong career.

The Dogs

The dogs are the ones that truly tell the story The dogs are the purpose and the reason for this whole adventure. So we will begin here with an introduction to the dogs. Like all of us, David and Betty named many of their old original dogs with northern sounding names. Once they decided to do the Iditarod, they also decided that the entire team should be given Alaskan type names. Therefore almost all of the younger dogs have names that can be found on a map of Alaska. The few exceptions may not be found on the map but can definitely be found in Alaska.

David and Betty's start for this grand endeavor began years ago when they first met, therefore when we talk about the dogs, it is only fitting to began with the...

Older canine members of the dream team.

Tundra was born February 12, 1985. His registered name is Snowy White Tundra, obviously named for his still lush and beautiful, all white coat. He is one of Betty and David's foundation dogs and was named before they started to use the Eskimo Bandit kennel name. He was an active member of the United States Champion Freight Race team. He ran in team position sometimes but usually he ran lead.

He has earned his Working Team Dog, WTD, Working Team Dog Excellent, WTDX titles and his back pack title, WPD.

He has helped to teach the new puppies tolerance from the day they were born. He has also participated in many public contact events from winter carnivals to school presentations. He was sure to give rides to any children who asked for them. "...and Yes," Betty says, "he knew what they were asking."

Tundra has also earned four points toward his AKC championship but his duties on the trail and elsewhere postponed his finishing.

Then, one day, a larger dog got into his pen and attacked him while no human was at home. True to his training not to fight, he refused to defend himself. When Betty arrived home and got the other dog out, she found Tundra terribly torn up. His front leg was broken and torn so badly it was hanging on mostly by a strip of skin. The leather of his nose was torn off as was one of his ears. He was cut and torn all over. His spirit however, was still strong as he helped Betty get him into the car for the rush to the veterinarian. Because he wasn't ready to give up, Betty refused to give up on him. She rejected the vet's suggestion to put him to sleep. The vet had quite a task to put him back together but he did his best. Tundra spent his long recovery period lying in the living room. Even today the lower portion of his right front leg doesn't quite point in the correct direction but it is a wonder that it is there at all. Of course he never returned to the show ring but he is still with Betty and David and gets daily walks on Alaskan trails.

He just celebrated his eighteenth birthday. He may be the oldest living Alaskan Malamute in North America.

Wrangell
(pronounced Rang-gell')

Wrangell was born May 10, 1989. His registered name is Eskimo Bandit's Wrangell. He was named for the Wrangell mountain range that runs along the Alaskan-Canadian border.

His thick black-tipped guard coat protects a rich golden undercoat.

Showing this beautiful boy in an area and at a time that sables were very rare, Betty was sometimes accused of bringing a dirty dog into the ring, but never by the judges who could see, smell, and touch him. He has earned both of his majors and, counting them, he holds fourteen points toward his AKC championship. Time constraints and his duties on the trail have added to the complications in his quest for that elusive one-last-point.

Betty says," Wrangell can do anything and with him I feel I can too." He is usually Betty's lead dog, often with a youngster beside him, learning to do the job also. He already has Ruby performing as a pretty good leader. He also helps to train all of the youngsters to harness and team.

Of the team training for the Iditarod, five are his own children and seven are his grandchildren.

Wrangell has such power even as a single leader that he has earned his Working Lead Dog WLD and his Working Lead Dog Excellent WLDX titles. Of course he holds his Working Team Dog WTD regular and Excellent WTDX titles also. He backpacks with Betty and David and holds his Working Pack Dog, WPD also. He has done weight pull competition with Betty for years. He not only holds his Working Weight pull

Dog, WWPD the regular and excellent, WWPDX titles but truth-be-known, he has qualified for over 50 WWPD legs. He also skijours and rollerblade jours and appears in parades and carnivals. One of his favorite activities is going to schools for educational programs for people.

Betty is right. He really does do it all!

***** News flash ! ! Wrangell finished his AKC Championship on June 22, 2002 !!!!!!!!

The AKC representative at the show that day said.... he believed that Wrangell is the oldest dog to achieve his championship!

He finished with a 3-point major!

Author's note: I was privileged to drive a team with Wrangell and his beautiful granddaughter Coleen as my lead team through the hills along the Alaska range.
I literally can't tell you how impressed I was by them and the whole team as well as the beauty of the whole experience. I will have to leave that up to the reader's imagination for now.

Seal and Talker
Seal and Talker are actually twins. They were born together in the same sac. So, I will start their story together as they did. They were born on May 30, 1989. Suntrana's Sutton Seal and Eskimo Bandit's Talker and their littermates were sold as puppies to a man who wanted them for his dog team. He seemed pleasant and sincere at the time. He agreed to the standard Eskimo Bandit contract. Good thing! The contract allows for drop-in home visits. Betty and David stopped by when the pups were a mere four months old. They were shocked and horrified to see the condition of their babies. They'd been beaten, burned, starved, and neglected. Betty and David called Animal Control and reported the cruelty. They took the puppies home. When the police came to the Britz's house that evening it wasn't to collect their statements. It was to arrest them for stealing the puppies!

Betty says now, "Well of course, we were blessed and they left the dogs with us after we paid a fine." They pursued the matter through proper legal channels. When the pups were a full year-and-a-half old they were finally legally the Britz's property again. Neither of them have ever regretted "breaking the law" and taking the pups while they could. They recovered quickly and have always been sweet and loving Malamutes. Kiana has a loving home. Bear Paw and Alaska both became search and rescue dogs and have very good homes.

Betty and David kept Wolf, Seal and Talker. Betty says of them "You would never think a human was so cruel to them. They are the best little Malamutes I can have. I'm proud of them."

 Both Seal and Talker were happy to become members of the Britz pleasure team which evolved into the U.S. Champion Freight Race Team and their Mid-Distance team. (Of course Wolf, too)

By the age of six months Seal was running lead. He grew so confident he could run either double or single lead. He earned not only his WLD, but his advanced title too, Working Lead Dog Excellent, WLDX. Of course he also has his WTD and WTDX, Working Team Dog Excellent titles also. He earned his Working Pack Dog, WPD, title by backpack hiking. He enjoys rollerjour and skijour activities. He was also tested and passed his examination for the AKC title of CGC, Canine Good Citizen. He, of course, helps to train the new pups. One of his favorite activities is bringing Santa to the mall by dog team to give the reindeer a rest.

Talker was also running lead for the team when he was six months old. He also has earned his Working Lead Dog (WLD) title. He has both his regular WTD and advanced Working Team Dog Excellent, WTDX titles. Backpacking with his canine and human family, he has earned his Working Pack Dog, WPD title. He has also passed the examination to earn the AKC title of Canine Good Citizen, CGC. Like his twin he rollerjours, skijours, and helps to train the youngsters. He used to be more quiet and less dominant than Seal, but in his maturity he has learned to go his own way as well. He wants to be his own canine. He loves to have his back rubbed and to go to schools to help give educational programs to young humans.

Ando

Eskimo Bandit's Ando was born December 24, 1991. He was such a beautiful pup that Betty and David decided to keep him. A musher came to them and said he was interested in owning Ando. The man said he had one malamute and would love to run a team of them. Ando would be perfect for his team. He promised to love Ando and take good care of him The man seemed so sincere that Betty and David finally said OK and Ando went off to his new home.

Almost three years later David and Betty received a telephone call from a veterinarian who knows that they do Alaskan Malamute rescue. He told them of a malamute that was injured, ill and malnourished The dog was in the vet's office at that time His owner told the veterinarian to go ahead and put him to sleep because he was too slow for the man's team of Alaskan huskies... even when he got his weight down to 40 - 45 pounds. The veterinarian asked Betty if they wanted him. Betty said, "yes" they'd be right down to get him The vet said to wait because he needed to do x-rays and an assessment of the dog's condition. When he called back fifteen minutes later he told them the dog had corn cobs lodged in his intestine and colon. He needed surgery to remove them. Later that evening, Betty and David went down to get him. He would complete his recovery with them in his new home.

They were shocked to find out that it was the beautiful puppy they had sold in good faith years ago. He knew them right away. His condition just broke Betty's heart. She told him he was coming home with mom and dad. His tail thumped as he licked Betty's hand.

They nursed him back to health. The next winter at his proper weight of ninety-six pounds he joined their mid-distance team.

To this day Betty is angry about the whole thing. She says that if she had her way, she'd like the mistreater to go through what he did to the dog. In lieu of that, she does her best to ensure it won't happen again. To protect her babies she has an extensive contract that is notarized and enforceable in District Court. She makes sure to do follow-up visits.

Meantime Ando has fully recovered and earned his Working Team Dog titles, both regular and excellent. Like the others he has also earned his Working Pack Dog, WPD and Working Weight pull Dog, WWPD titles. He also ski-jours and rollerblade-jours. He helps train youngsters and has earned his AKC Canine Good Citizen, CGC title.

He enjoys participating in educational programs and bringing Santa to the mall. (Oh those lucky well-rested reindeer!)

Properly treated he has made a complete comeback and proven his quality.

Eskeimo

Eskimo Bandit's Eskeimo was born February 10, 1992. Betty calls him her "true black beauty". He only needs one major to finish his AKC championship. He has been too busy to get back into the show ring lately though. He has earned his Working Weight Pull title, his Working Weight pull Excellent title, and his backpack title. He has also passed the examination and earned his AKC title, Canine Good Citizen.

He accompanies Betty to the library for story time and dog education for the children. He is a regular for visits to medical care facilities and schools. Everyone always mentions how beautiful he is. Of course he does his part helping to train the new puppies as well!

Once he and Betty were hiking on a warm autumn day. Betty's blood sugar became low. She said to Eskie, "Momma can't make it" and sat down on the ground to take out a bit of candy to correct the problem. Eskeimo sat down on her, then he lay down on top of her. They were eye to eye. As Betty tells it, "I was warm, but a little smushed. I ate my candy. He got off of me when I felt better."

**Another News Flash!! This summer Eskeimo finished his AKC Championship also!

 **Chena** (pronounced Shee' - nah) Eskimo Bandit's Cheena was born on February 10, 1992. This beautiful rich gray and white is Betty's very frequent companion They do many things together and thoroughly enjoy each others' company. Besides helping to teach the puppies, she keeps active doing obedience, hiking, bicycling and going to dog shows. Betty gives demonstrations in dog obedience and training. Chena is her partner in these school and public contacts. She has earned her Working Team Dog, Working Pack Dog, and Working Weight pull Dog titles as well as her AKC Canine Good Citizen title and one leg toward her Companion Dog, another AKC title. She has been a wonderful mother. She also feels it's her job to take care of Betty. She was Betty's lead dog on one of the teams that she drove in to the first cabin in Alaska. *...More about that later.*

Kobuk

Eskimo Bandit Kobuk Britz was born June 29, 1993. This very dark gray and white beauty is full of spice and vinegar. He is a delightful combination of energy and mischief. Once at a national specialty in Minnesota, David was showing him in the bred by exhibitor class. He decided to act like a clown. He was looking and talking to everyone. He would even go up on his hind legs to wave his forepaws as if to say, "Look at me!" David finally got him to stay on the floor and they gaited down the mat. After the turnaround they got about halfway back to the judge. He suddenly jumped up on David's hip, hung on and humped. The whole crowd laughed. Betty commented, "I thought David would never show again! Kobuk, I think, hoped so too. He would rather be on the trails." He still got the 3rd Place ribbon. The judge said he liked the dog but he felt that Kobuk needed more experience in the ring.

He has earned: Working Team Dog, Working Team Dog Excellent, his Working Weight Pull Dog, and his Working Pack Dog. He has AKC points toward his conformation championship. He was also the youngest dog to enter and complete the "midnight run".

He sired seven of the puppies on the dream team and of course has had a very big paw in their training.

Ruby

Keikewabic Eskimo Bandit Ruby was born April 24, 1997. This lovely red and white girl was born in Canada and has her CKC and AKC registrations. Her name has two meanings. She was named for the town in Alaska but also for the precious red gem that she looks so much like.

As Betty tells it, "We were so excited to get Ruby! We

have had a name for a red for years. We went to Keikewabic kennels in Dryden,Ontario, Canada to get her. Maureen Andersen and her daughter love their dogs very much. You can tell by watching as we did while we stayed with them.

Ruby Red, as we call her, became a United States citizen on March 23, 2000. We had a big party for her. The dogs had meatloaf-with-cheese-frosting cake. When we went to a Chicagoland dog show, people told us that the judges didn't like reds. She won 1st place in Sweepstakes and 2nd place in Open.

Ruby loves to run on the team. Wrangell taught her to be a leader. She gave rides at Hancock school, my godchild's birthday party, and has appeared in many parades. She even helped a friend drive her team at the Calumet Heritage Day parade of 2001"

Ruby has earned her Working Team Dog, Working Pack Dog, and Canine Good Citizen titles. She also has points toward her AKC conformation championship.

Ruby had seven puppies last year. They were sired by Kobuk. They are all in training as part of the Iditarod Dream Team.

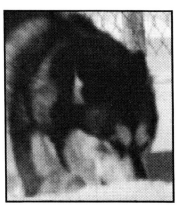

Nanook

Nanook Rose of the North was born on February 14, 1998. This black and white girl came to the Britz's in the spring of 2000. Betty talks about Nanook, saying, "She was lacking in a lot of areas." She was very leggy, thin-boned, and had a poor coat. Our veterinarian gave her the nickname "wild woman" because of her behavior. She was dog aggressive, also food and toy aggressive. She thought we were all dogs and it was OK to play rough with us. She was just a big foolish kid who didn't know any better. Delores, who brought her to us, said that "You have your work cut out for you." She was right. It took time and work and patience. We put her on top quality food, a good vitamin mineral supplement and started her in obedience. Now she is a different dog. She has developed and matured physically into a very attractive young lady. She is very well behaved and has people manners."

On February 2, 2001, Nanook gave birth to a five-puppy litter, that was sired by Wrangell. They are part of the all AKC registered Alaskan Malamute Iditarod Dream Team.

Nanook, herself, had to postpone her training to be on the dream team for a season. In January 2002, she delivered a seven-puppy litter while at the first cabin in Alaska.

Aurora

Eskimo Bandit's Aurora was born May 16, 1999. This beautiful gray and white female loves everyone. Betty says, "Even though she is ours, we feel Aurora is the perfect malamute and many others have told us so

22

also."

Like so many of David and Betty's dogs it seems that she does everything. She is a sweet and loving with people. She also gets along with other dogs and bitches. She works hard and she shows well. In very limited showing she has already picked up her first two points toward an AKC conformation championship. She already has her AKC Canine Good Citizen title. She has her Working Weight Pull Dog title. She has Working Team Dog and has earned one leg toward her Working Team Dog Excellent that has been documented as of this writing. She has actually done the work required but it has gone undocumented because she is often the lead on training runs with David now that they are in Alaska. Hopefully before this book goes to print she may even have finished earning her WTDX.

Once when she was with Betty at a weight pull contest in Denmark, Wisconsin, Aurora did Betty a big favor. Throughout the day, after their turn at pulling the weight, Betty and Aurora exited the contest area and turned to the left. They climbed over a small hill. On the other side they were out of sight from everyone. In relative privacy Betty could reward Aurora with a brief off-leash playful romp.

As the day wore on Betty became progressively more tired. She was so busy visiting with friends that she only gets to see occasionally, that she failed to realize that her blood sugar level was dropping. The amounts of the weights were going up. She was expending more energy encouraging Aurora to pull. Each turn required more time and effort. Betty failed to notice that she was no longer thinking clearly. Another turn to pull came around. Aurora almost ran to Betty with the heavy weight. Leaving the pull area she hauled Betty to the right instead of to the left... and straight into the refreshment tent. It was only then that it dawned on Betty just how weak and disoriented she really was. She got a snack and quickly remedied her low blood sugar problem. Later she confided that if they had gone left over the hill to play in the field...

she would probably still be there.

She also earned a leg toward her Working Weight Pull Dog Excellent that. Aurora and Betty have a very special bond.

Artic

Wolfsong's Earth, Wind and Fire was born May 24, 2000. This handsome black and white boy is a real lover. Betty says, he's "built like a rock and loves to work. Artic is a rough-neck and he loves to play." He went with David and Betty to the Baraga, MI, Fair. A weight pull is held to entertain and educate the fairgoers. The weight limited to 1000 pounds, because this is held in the heat of the summer. The event doesn't start until nine pm so the cooler evening air is present but that makes for a rather late night. The late hour is another reason for the weight limit. Artic was entered in this event for his first contest ever. He weighed 90 pounds at that time and did an excellent job pulling all the way through the 1000 pound round. Now that he is in Alaska he enjoys running in either team or wheel position.

Gateway

Wolfsong's Gateway to Nome was born November 8, 2000. This black and white boy is very outstanding in appearance. People who don't know any better have accused David of running a Greenland Eskimo dog in with his malamutes. Most people don't recognize his color pattern as being normal for an Alaskan malamute. For a while in our breed's history, it was common practice for a breeder to drop a puppy marked as he is into a water bucket when he was born. The standard of the breed even refers to splash-coated coloring as undesirable. Gateway's breeder does not believe in destroying a healthy puppy for cosmetic reasons. David and Betty agree with that point of view. In fact they say they find the coloring attractive. When the author was discussing this with Betty and David they pointed out the fact that undesirable is not even a fault. It is just a matter of opinion. They said they consider the information contained in the paragraph that begins "IMPORTANT.— In judging Alaskan malamutes their function as a sledge dog for heavy freighting must be given consideration above all else." as much greater value They selected Gateway for his structure and movement. If he had been a more traditional color, he would have been "pick of the litter".

When he was born, his breeder started calling him Gateway after the boxes the well-known computers come in. It started as a joke, but he learned his name and responded well to it. David liked the name but all of the youngsters on the team have been named after something that can be found on a map of Alaska (or in Alaska). David searched the map but could find nothing that sounded even remotely like Gateway. Finally an enterprising person suggested the name Gateway to Nome to represent the famous huge wooden gateway that the dog teams finishing the Iditarod must pass beneath. Betty says she would love to do some commercials for Gateway computers with her boy.

He loved his obedience classes and has earned his Canine Good Citizen, CGC title. He is an excellent wheel dog and has been doing some training for the lead position. He knows he is special.

Q.T. (Cutie)
Wolfsong's Quick Tok was born November 8, 2000. This gray and white is a little pistol. She is very good with the other girls. She is like everybody's little mother. Betty says of her, "When we go for walks she always checks up on me, never going far

from me. She was unsure about working on the sled so we took a tire for her to pull around the yard. She is doing much better. She will run team at first. If she gets confidence she could learn to run lead. I will put her point for practice when she has gained some more confidence." QT loves food and can be a little stinker about it sometimes. She does very well in obedience and has her Canine Good Citizen CGC title."

Rainy

"He is supposed to be named Rainy Pass but he is CKC registered as Marlayne's Rainpath. This gray and white was born on December 26, 2000. He's a go-getter who really enjoys running team. He did well in his obedience class and has earned his canine good citizen CGC title. He loves to have his butt and ears rubbed. He is big and hopefully will become a power wheel dog on our team."

Golovin

Marlayne's Golovin was born December 26, 2000. Betty calls this big gray and white boy "Go love in'". They got him from Portage La Prairie, Canada. He and his brother Rainy were shy when they first came to Betty and David so

they took them to town very often for a lot of socialization. Golovin did excellently in his obedience class. He has earned Canine Good Citizen, CGC title. Betty says, "He is a mush mush boy, big and lovable so his name fits him."

Kechi

Eskimo Bandit Kechikan was born February 2, 2001. She is the daughter of Wrangell and Nanook. Although this black and white girl looks a little bit leggy (it could be her age), she shows absolutely amazing power running either wheel or team position. Brimming with enthusiasm, she is out-standingly happy-go-lucky.

Galena

Eskimo Bandit's Galena
Is another black and white daughter of Wrangell and Nanook, also born February 2, 2001. She is a big powerful girl who runs a strong wheel position. She can run any position in the team. When she runs in the lead she has shown excellent ability at finding and following a trail. Although she is not cuddly-kissy like her brothers she is still very affectionate and likes to be touched and rubbed.

Grayling

Eskimo Bandit's Grayling is the only gray son of Wrangell and Nanook. His name is a mere coincidence because he was born black as were his brothers and sisters.

He was named before his color changed. He is from the February 2, 2001, litter. Sometimes he runs lead. Sometimes he runs team. He is a big lover who likes to give kisses.

Elim

Eskimo Bandit's Elim, a black and white son of Wrangell and Nanook, was born on February 2, 2001. Another good sized male, he often runs wheel or team. He is a big sweet baby known for his boundless enthusiasm for everything and everybody. Happy-go-lucky, he likes to jump up and kiss people on top of the head. (This can make it very difficult to take photographs or videos of ongoing action, but he is so cute and silly that no one really cares.)

* Watch for him in the epilogue

Nikolai

Eskimo Bandit's Nikolai is the fifth big powerful offspring of Wrangell and Nanook from the February 2, 2001, litter. This attractive black and white fellow usually runs wheel. He is a very solid worker with a very sweet soft personality. He gets along happily

with everyone. This makes him a very good dog to put some-one who is unsure, next to. David often uses this young fellow to help teach other dogs.

Iditarod

Eskimo Bandit Iditarod was born to Kobuk and Ruby January 30, 2001. This seal and white boy works hard and loves it. When he was a youngster David thought he might be too small for the team. But when David saw him work he changed his mind. He is a little power train. He turned the Britz's 300 lb. three-wheeled cart sideways the first time David told him to hike. He often runs in the wheel position. He can run lead but is still working on building confidence. He loves to swim and to play with his buddy, Timber, a wire-haired pointer.

Alaska

Eskimo Bandit Alaska iLI was born to Kobuk and Ruby January 30, 2001. (iLI is an Inuit word that means to-be-like.) This lovely seal and white male is almost identical to his brother, Iditarod. He was named after his grandmother so he has big paws to fill, which he has already started doing. He is an excellent wheel or team member— always having his line tight. Alaska is quiet and easygoing.

Taylor

Eskimo Bandit's Taylor is another Kobuk and Ruby baby that was born January 30, 2001. This pretty little gray and white female looks very much like her three grey sisters but she is very much an individual. She is an excellent team dog and a hard worker. She gives her all, all of the time. David calls her a little fireball.

Delta

Eskimo Bandit's Delta Jct is almost identical in looks to her sister Taylor... and to her other two sisters. She is just as much an individual as the rest. She loves to please and very much enjoys running on the team. She is a very good wheel dog.

Suntrana

Eskimo Bandit's Suntrana iLI, is another one of the four nearly identical gray girls from Kobuk and Ruby, and is a very special individual. She has big paws to fill because she was named after her great grandmother, a world record-holding weight puller, (remember iLI means to-be-like?) She did very well in obedience class and loves to do any kind of work. She will be a leader. She is already running lead sometimes with her father, Kobuk or her aunt, Aurora. She also runs point. There is never slack in her tugline. Suntrana is very playful and happy go lucky.

Coleen

Eskimo Bandit's Coleen is a pretty little gray and white female from Kobuk and Ruby. She was born January 30, 2001. She can run any position on the team but she is in training for lead. She

will be a very strong leader when she gains practice and confidence. She is already quite good with commands and is very responsive to praise. (This author can vouch for her enthusiasm on the trail!) She is very lovable and a good worker.

Brook

Eskimo Bandit's Brooks is the only black and white youngster from the litter from Kobuk and Ruby. She runs point position right now and is very good at it.

She did well in obedience training. She loves to wear the lime green harness that her aunt Delores made for her. It shows up beautifully against her shiny black coat. David and Betty tell her how beautiful she is and she knows it and stands proudly. Brook loves to explore and to go swimming. She runs lead very well. She likes to be out front. She has bright eyes and a strong will.

Kotzebue

Windy City's Kotzebue was born just outside Chicago, Illinois, on July 22, 2001. That made this splashy little gray and white female the youngest member of the expedition to Alaska. As if the whole group was not cuddly and lovable enough, she added even more cuddliness and a healthy touch of baby innocence.

I am sure she is one of David's favorites. This was especially apparent when it was time to put the the dogs back into the truck. She only weighed about 30 pounds. When she was on his shoulder wrapped around his head, it was more of a cuddle of affection than anything else. She was also a terrific motivating factor when it came to dogs playing with each other on the picket line along the way.

Idita-puppies

These little guys were Nanook and Artic's rather unplanned surprise for this adventure. They were invisible as Nanook smuggled seven extra little tiny malamutes through Canada to Alaska. They were finally visible when they were born at the Vaughan's cabin in January of 2002.

All of the Idita-puppies have been named after creeks in Alaska. Trapper and Willow have gone to live in their new home in Michigan. The rest of them; Wolf, Canyon, Stoney, Cache, and Bunco are still with Betty and David as of this writing.

There are three more canines that need to be mentioned before we leave this chapter.

Dehlia

Lady Delilah's Over the Lee is a Pembroke Welsh Corgi that was born May 4, 1998. She came to Betty as a rescue. Doug later adopted her and she became his constant companion. She is playful and feisty and gets along well with most of the malamutes. I was personally surprised to discover just how tough this little dog is. She fared just fine traveling in a box in the dog truck, and is quite happy living outside with the big dogs.

(Now writing becomes more difficult.)

Wolf

Eskimo Bandit's Knight Wolf was born May 30, 1989. (The rest of Wolf's section is presented here quite directly as Betty wrote it, on December 14, 2001) "Wolf has always had a gentle spirit and a quiet peaceful

howl. He has run lead and team on our US Champion freight team. He also ran on our mid-distance team. In one competition he was drugged by someone. (The rest of the team, too) He was so affected that he ran right past mom (me) at the finish and fell down in the parking lot. The vet came and did blood work. He said that Wolf and the team had been drugged with an overdose of dramamine. Wolf was so overdosed that he would probably die. I'll never forget that day! The veterinarian was surprised that Wolf survived. He said any other dog would be dead.

In 1990 he had his first cancer, (myloma). We were told he would only live six months. In 1999, he had his second cancer,(testicular). We had them removed and he bounced back again. Throughout this he still continued to give rides, love and education to children and to puppies, both of which he always loved.

Our Wolf died on this trip. It nearly broke us, mind, body and spirit. We knew the other fur kids and many malamute people are counting on us, otherwise we would have turned around and gone back home. That night we were quiet. We prayed. Tundra was not doing well also. The next morning Tundra was running around like a kid again. The day was warm and sunny. I knew that Wolf with his gentle, loving spirit was with us and we should go forward with his spirit. So we are. When you think of Wolf remember his drive and heart never to quit but also remember his other side that I have seen so often. His gentle, loving, patient, and soft howling spirit."

Eskimo Bandit's Knight Wolf
WTD, WTDX, WPD, WWPD, CGC
5-30-89 to 12-13-01

Isis
Eskimo Bandit's Isis was born on December 19, 1987. This beautiful black and white girl is all the more striking because of the brightness of her open white face. Betty calls her ice, wind and fire. She explains, "This fits her   all around personality.

To some dogs she is as cold as ice. She moves like the wind. To people she is like a warm fire on a freezing day."

She has earned 12 points, including one major, toward her AKC conformation championship. She also earned two legs for her Companion Dog, CD title. She already had her CGC. She also possessed her backpacking title, WPD.

Isis celebrated her 14th birthday on this trip.

She passed away in the Yukon Territory of Canada near the end of the trip. It was another terrible blow to every one.

Eskimo Bandit's Isis CGC, WPD
12-19-87 to 12-21-01

*Crystal Bandit
the Foundation*

*Suntrana
Weight Pull*

Idita Puppies at Play

The First Race

The first race from Anchorage to Nome was by far the most important one. Instead of prize money..human life was what the race was run for!

The first one was also the fastest. Anchorage to Nome in under 7 days.

It doesn't count like the Anchorage to Nome race of today because the first 298 miles were done by railroad train. Also, no individual completed the total distance. The only one to go the whole distance in the first run was a little 20 pound package of serum, wrapped in a quilt and a layer of canvas.... and later, along the trail, a fur covering was added.

OK, ok... Let's start at the beginning. In January of 1925, Dr. Curtis Welch, the only doctor in the town of Nome, Alaska, discovered the beginning of an epidemic of diphtheria. He had lost the first two victims to it even before he could confirm a diagnosis. Though he correctly confirmed it with the third case, he lost that patient too. They were all children.

Dr. Welch had only a small supply of antitoxin for diphtheria on hand and it was 5 years old. It might not be effective. Even if it were, there was not enough of it to stop the illness already started and immunize everyone else who was exposed.

Dr. Welch sent out an urgent message on the wireless. It was a plea for help.

Nome at that time was virtually cut off from the rest of the world in the wintertime when boat traffic was impossible. The only exceptions were the wireless and the mail, which was brought in by a relay of dogsleds.

The nearest supply of the desperately needed, life-saving serum was in Anchorage, close to 1,000 miles away.

One of the people to respond to Dr. Welch's plea was Alaskan Governor Scott C. Bone. He immediately authorized a special run on the (then new) Alaska Railroad to take the serum north. The railroad ran to Fairbanks not to Nome, however. Even if the train brought the serum about 300 miles north...It still needed to go about 700 miles to the west. The question was how to move it. It was a relatively small package, weighing only about 20 pounds. Size and weight weren't a consideration. Distance and weather were.

In 1925, flying was still in its infancy. Cold weather flying, as in Alaska, was non-existent. Most airplanes still had open cockpits. Airplanes in Alaska were usually dissembled and warehoused for the winter months. Even so, the possibility had to be considered. If a highly qualified pilot could get a reliable plane to use, he might be able to fly the serum from Fairbanks to Nome in very short order. The question was, even if both were available, how sure could anyone be that a plane could fly over the mountains. The thin air and severely low temperatures could interfere with a machine's ability to operate. They might also disable even the toughest of pilots. The serum would do no good if it were sitting in a crumpled airplane somewhere on the side of a mountain

Gov. Bone decided to go with dogteams. The mail had been getting through to Nome with considerable regularity. It usually took a parcel almost a month to get there. With excellent dogteams, careful timing, and the head start the railroad could give perhaps the normal time could be cut in half. Nome might be able to receive the serum in only 15 days.!

On Monday, January 26, 1925 the train pulled out of Anchorage carrying the precious 20 pound bundle. The cylindrical container was wrapped in a quilt and then canvas. Conductor Frank Knight accepted the responsibility for the package for the first 298 miles of its amazing journey.

At 11:00 Tuesday night, Frank Knight handed the bundle over to "Wild Bill" Shannon, the first musher in this incredible relay race at a town called Nenana located on the Tanana River. Shannon secured the bundle on his sled and headed his team of 9 malamutes right down that river.

By noon the following day, he arrived at the roadhouse at Tolovana to turn the bundle over to Dan Green. He had covered the first 52 miles of the trek. The two men talked about the seriousness of the situation in Nome while they warmed the package with the serum in the building. Then Green headed for Manley Hot Springs...31 miles away.

There he met with Johnny Folger, a Tanana Indian. Together they warmed the bundle in the roadhouse there. Then Folger headed his team for Fish Lake, 28 miles down the river.

When he turned the bundle over to Sam Joseph, an Indian of the Athabaskan Nation, it had a fur wrapping as an additional protection against the cold. After the partial unwrapping and warmup time, Joseph headed his team of 7 malamutes out. They made the 26 mile run to Tanana in 2hrs and 40 minutes.

There after the warming, Titus Nickolai, another Indian, and his team took the package and ran to Kallands, 34 miles further along.

Nickolai turned the serum over to Dave Corning who ran it the 24 miles to the shelter house at Nine Mile in about 3 hours time.

He warmed it and turned it over to Edgar Kalland who made the 30 mile run to Kokrines.

There Harry Pitka, a man of partial Indian descent, accepted it and ran his 7 dog team the 30 mile distance to Ruby averaging better than 9 miles per hour.

At Ruby, Bill McCarty using the dogs of Alex Brown with a dog named Prince in the lead, took the bundle and ran the 28 miles to Whiskey Creek.

At about 10 pm Thursday, he handed-off to Edgar Nollner, who was relying on his 8-year old lead dog Dixie to inspire his team. She must have done a good job of it because the 7 big grey malamutes swept down the trail to Galena...24 miles away.

There George Nollner, Edger's older brother, took the package and made the 18 mile run to Bishop Mountain. The two brothers had covered 42 miles in less than 6 hours.

Charlie Evans, the 22 year old son of a white trader

and an Indian mother, took the package inside and warmed it for nearly an hour before leaving with it at 5 am to run his 9 dog team the next 30 miles.

At the Indian village of Nulato, Evans handed the serum over to Tommy Patsy, a Koyukuk Indian. He was driving a team of the best dogs in the village. He made the 36 miles to Kaltag in only 3 and one half hours. That was the last run on the river which had long ago merged with and become the mighty Yukon River.

The serum had come 390 miles along the valleys and rivers since leaving the train. There had been temperatures of -60 degrees to -30 degrees. There had been winds of 40 mph and more. Snowstorms, darkness, blizzards...none of it had kept these intrepid men and their dogteams from doing their best to help people in need.

Now the trail was changing. Climbs and drops through hills, mountains and passes...and then along the seacoast and even out onto the sea ice....each with its own variety of incredible weather and hazards.

At Kaltag a small powerful Indian known along the Yukon as Jackscrew received the package and headed up and over the mountains between there and the sea. Starting at 9:10 pm Friday, he drove his team the 40 miles to Old Woman in a little over 6 hours.

Victor Anagick, an Eskimo, picked up the serum at 3:30 Saturday afternoon and drove a team of 11 dogs that belonged to his employer, Charles Traeger, the 34 remaining miles to Unalakleet, and the sea...Norton Sound.

Myles Gonangnan, another Eskimo, took the bundle and headed north through the foothills along the coast with his team of 8 mixed breed dogs. Most of the way they were breaking their own trail through 6" of new snow. When after 25 miles he stopped a Eban to warm the serum, he emerged back outside to a snowstorm which he battled the last 15 miles of his leg of the trip He covered his 40 miles at an average speed of 4 to 5 hard-fought miles per hour but he never wavered.

At Shaktolik, Gonangnan turned the serum over to Henry Ivanoff a part Russian, part Eskimo man. Just out of town he had serious trouble with his team. While he was untangling them he saw Leonhard Seppala, a well known winner of many dogsled races, and his famous team of Siberian huskies. He passed by, going in the opposite direction. Seppala was on his way to Nulato where he thought he'd meet with the serum. He had been on the trail and therefore missed the communications that there were more teams and drivers involved and the precious package was traveling faster than anticipated.

Henry Ivanoff had to wave the tough little Norseman down and make him turn around. They both knew that Seppala's team led by Scotty and the famous Togo would be the faster of the two.

The package was transferred to his sled and he headed back the way he had just come. To shave off miles and time, Seppala chose to cross the ice at the mouth of Norton Bay. Despite winds and a snowstorm, he trusted his determined leaders to take him through. They didn't fail him. A little before 8 o'clock on Saturday night he arrived in Isaac's Point on the north shore of the Bay. There he rested while the serum warmed. Early Sunday morning he drove his team out into a blizzard to continue the trip. This time he took the shore trail on the advice of an old Eskimo. Good thing too because the wild winds had caused a breakup of the ice he traveled beside. Even the ice he had crossed just yesterday had broken up and gone out to sea.

At a roadhouse in Golovin, Seppala turned the serum over to a sourdough named Charlie Olson. After the warming, he headed out into the teeth of the storm. The wind was so wild that several times Olson and his team of 7 malamutes were physically blown right off of the trail, landing in a heap in the unpacked snow. Every time it happened he untangled everyone and with the help of his faithful leader Jack, regained the trail and continued.

With terrific effort he managed to traverse the 25 miles

to Bluff where he met with Gunnar Kaasen who was driving a team of Seppala's Siberians. They were led by a dog named Balto. Seppala hadn't cared much for him as a leader because he seemed to lack the fire and drive of Seppala's favorite, Togo. Kaasen liked him for his steady determination. That was what was needed to face the blizzard they had to get through.

He was only supposed to drive the 13 dog team to Point Safety and meet with Ed Rohn and his racing team. For reasons that are now lost in time, he continued on past there.

At 5:30 am Monday, February 2, 1925, he drove down Front Street of a still-sleeping Nome.

The serum had come the 674 miles by dogsled in 127.5 hours!

The epidemic was stopped. There were no more deaths and the quarantine was lifted on February 21...exactly one month from the start.

The author has intended no offense with the use of some of the terms contained herein. They were applied according to the information contained in the references that were available. We know that most of the 20 drivers were of Native American descent...but then again the term American is also not a native word.

Iditarod

Iditarod is a place along the Iditarod River in southwestern Alaska. In the early 1900's it was a goldrush boom town. Today it is a ghost town. Every other year it is inhabited by people who have come there for the race that bears its name.

The Iditarod Trail is one that ran from the seaports of Seward and Anchorage to the town of Iditarod and later all the way to Nome. It was one of the main supply trails during the goldrush era. When the goldrush faded so did it. By the mid-1900's it was virtually unused and pretty much forgotten.

In 1964 Dorothy G. Page was the chairperson of the Wasilla-Knick Centennial celebration. The committee was already formed and working on plans to celebrate 100 years since the purchase of Alaska from Russia back in 1867.

One of the things Dorothy Page wanted to do was to celebrate the rugged Alaskan spirit. She felt that dogsledding was a vital part of that heritage. She was also aware of the old dogsled freighting trail that ran right through Wasilla and neighboring Knick. She believed that a dogsled race down the old Iditarod trail and back would be just what she had in mind.

She suggested the idea to Joe Redington Sr. and his wife Vi. They had arrived and settled in Alaska many years ago and were well known in the dogsledding community. They were all for it and immediately pitched in with everything they could to make such a race happen, and be successful.

The first Iditarod Trail race was run in 1967. There were mushers from all over Alaska and even two from Massachusetts. That relatively short race (approximately 27 miles long) was won by Isaac Okleasik from Teller, Alaska, and his team of large working dogs.

That basic race was run again in 1969.

Page and the Redingtons wanted to see the race expanded. Their next goal was to have the race run all the way to the old town of Iditarod in 1973.

BUT in 1972 the U.S. Army reopened the whole trail as part of a winter training exercise.

A serious discussion was held and the decision was made to go the entire distance of over 1000 miles....all the way to Nome. That first full distance race in 1973 saw 22 mushers finish.

Since 1983 the ceremonial start of the race has been from downtown Anchorage. There is an official re-start the following day...usually from the airport at Wasilla.

Since that first finish in 1973, there have been between 400 and 500 mushers to complete the race. They have come from many other states and from quite a variety of different countries.

Now the race has two routes over which it is run. On odd numbered years the race sticks to the old Iditarod trail. On even numbered years however, the racers turn north when they leave Ophir. They follow the trail that takes them through Cripple to Ruby on the bank of the Yukon River. There they follow the river and the trail taken by the mushers that ran the life-saving serum to Nome in 1925. At Kaltag both the old Iditarod trail (now also called the southern route) and the newer (?) northern route unite and become one for the rest of the way to Nome.

This author doesn't have the official explanation of why this is done but she is sure that each route commemorates the rugged and heroic spirit of the true Alaska!

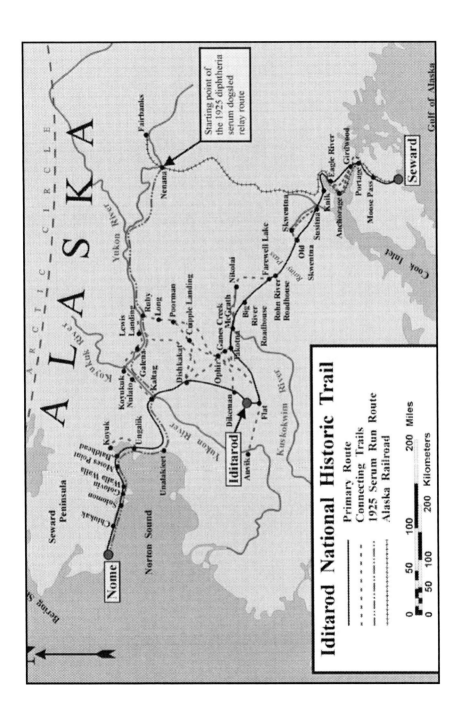

Iditarod National Historic Trail

43

The Breed(s)

The Alaskan malamute is the only breed of dog that evolved totally on the North American continent. There are other breeds that were developed in this country but they all came from breeds of dogs that already existed in other countries.

The Alaskan malamute was developed and maintained by a tribe of native American that lived along Kotzebue Sound since long before the white man's arrival.

Their purpose in life was to survive and to aid in the survival of their owners, the people of the Mahlmuit tribe. This was later to be pronounced "Malamute" by the white man and became recognized as the name of both the people and their dogs. Together they trans-

ported this nomadic tribe's possessions. The dogs were developed for power and efficiency not speed. Their evolution into animals that could do the job and survive in the climate of that part of the world did have one interesting side effect. They are also probably the most beautiful breed of dog in the world.

Most of the time the Mahlmuit people worked right alongside the dogs as they traveled. Because of this there was no great need for speed. A man or a woman walking next to the dog and pulling the sledge loaded with the family's entire possessions just wanted to get where the group of them wanted to be next, whether it was a hunting camp or a tribal meeting. Most of these families only owned a few dogs...just enough to get the job done.

With the advent of the white man on the Alaskan scene, the role of the dogs changed in some ways and in other ways it remained pretty much the same.

The white man wanted to drive his dogs and be able to ride on the sled. With the French trader the word "Marche" meaning "to go" appeared. It was later corrupted into the ever-popular "mush!" Later the gold rush brought farmers from the midwest of the lower 48. They brought along terms that they used for driving their mules. "Gee" for a right turn, "Haw" for a left turn, and of course the very common (and often ignored by a fresh team) "Whoa".

The practice of riding on the sled and the fact that the white man usually had an awful lot to carry along necessitated powerful teams. (It seems that the white man has never been able to get along on as little as the native in whatever environment he ventures.) The dogs of the Mahlmuit tribe were in great demand for heavy transport through rough country. With the large influx of white man that the gold rush brought also came a large influx of just about any kind of dog that could be obtained. Some of them worked out, some...no many of them were interbred with the dogs already in the North. Enterprising people even imported dogs from northern tribes in areas of what is now Russia. These were what we now recognize as Siberian huskies and Samoyeds. Because they were smaller and lighter, it usually took more of them to equal the power of the Malamute. They did have more speed, however.

This became more important with the growing popularity of racing. Later they would be replaced by mixed-breed dogs bred for even more speed. For a while the pure Northern breed dogs seemed to be in danger of disappearing altogether. Dog fanciers in the lower 48 got the breeds recognized by the American kennel Club in the mid 1930's and have worked to preserve them since.

So basically we have some breeds of dogs that run in the snow and pull sleds. Since more people are familiar with horses than are familiar with the Northern breeds, I will try to explain them in equine comparisons.

The Alaskan Malamute is like the large and powerful beer-wagon horses we see nowadays on the commercials.

The Siberian husky and the Samoyed are like Arabian horses...small, light, faster and usually hotter blooded.

The animal called the Alaskan Husky is actually a mix of breeds ...Northern breeds crossed with something else that is faster. This is very much like the American Thoroughbred....a mixture of Arabian and Barb horses with local other horses to create a leggier animal with even greater speed.

Now you could hook Arabians or Thoroughbreds to a big beer wagon and if you used enough of them they could certainly pull that wagon (though maybe not as calmly and steadily as the big boys). You could also take the Budweiser Clydesdales down to Churchill Downs and run them. They would certainly be able to run around the track...just not as swiftly as the hot bloods. (I always said if it were done it would be a good idea to take along a newspaper and a chair to be comfortable waiting for them to finish.)

As for the different dogs and the Iditarod.....

Over 1,000 miles of rough terrain, even pulling a light sled....It wouldn't really level the playing field....but it might bring them a little closer.

46

Leaving

December 6, 2001

Well... it has begun. Not with a flourish... but with a lot of frustration. BUT, frustration overcome by pure determination. *(As we were to find out, that was going to be a huge factor in this whole endeavor).*

My part in this grand adventure is purely supportive... and very limited... some groceries and odds and end things... and help with their transportation. That is what has started... slowly... very slowly... with a severe and stubborn paperwork clog. *(We were later to learn that there was probably a very good reason for the problems that we were having at this start.)*

The man at the truck rental place was very pleasant and worked hard all day to get the mess straightened out and me on the road, but the problem, or at least part of it, was the fact that we lost a valuable day for travel.

We wrestled with paperwork and the computer information. And the fact that none of the proper facts were being communicated. The deal that David had made over the phone, appeared to be non-existent. Many strange things seemed to go wrong. We were in sporadic telephone contact with David and Betty up in Michigan. Poor David was running all over three different towns to coordinate what he needed to. We finally got to the point that I could go out and look over the truck. On the telephone and in person both David and I had mentioned the fact that we would be driving through the Canadian Rockies. As I looked over the truck, I asked if it would be capable of doing the job we needed. The leasor of the truck adjusted my rear view mirrors and assured me that this truck would be just fine. When I noticed that there was only one 50 gallon diesel fuel tank and asked if that would be sufficient, he told me that I could install another one if I wanted to. I thought that was a strange remark.

We finally had everything ready to go. As I pulled the truck forward the man called to me that if we had any problems on the road we should just dial the 800 number that was painted in numbers over 1 ft. tall on the side of the truck.

By the time I drove the lumbering vehicle out of the lot and onto the road in northern Illinois it was too late for me to get to New Holstein, WI to pick up the dog food. Instead I headed for Waterford, WI. I was hoping to make it in time. I wanted to pick up the barrels we had ordered for storage and to become dog houses. Most factories close 3:30 PM. I rolled out of the truck rental just after 2:30. At first I had to take it a little easy as I got used to the strange vehicle. I headed out, driving through afternoon traffic. 3:00 came and went. I kept driving. 3:15 PM... it was still quite a distance away. 3:30 I was still one small town away. Rather than turn and go home, I decided to see if anyone was staying late. I continued on to the industrial park, drove in, and parked, though a little awkwardly. I climbed down from the high cab of the truck and headed for the office door. The service door opened and the woman who was in charge of getting the barrels assembled and ready for me to pick up, pointed to the loading dock. We had the barrels loaded and stacked no time at all. I was thrilled! Not only were the people there and wonderfully helpful, but the invoice was addressed to: "Iditarod Team" it was the first time I had seen it in writing by a totally objective outsider.

It is Real! It has begun!

December 8, 2001

I drove up here yesterday. On the way I stopped in New Holstein, Wisconsin, and picked up four pallets full of dog food. David and Betty have been preparing for the trip and are still in the process. The dogs all look wonderful! I took a lot of pictures to send to Sharon so she can put them on the Internet. The Britz's received a big bag of T-shirts in the mail. They were donated by the printer, Favorite Silk Screen and Embroidery. On the front they say Eskimo Bandit and have a

48

picture of their logo. On the reverse side, it says Iditarod Dream Team, and below AKC Alaskan Malamute. Underneath, it gives the Eskimo Bandit web site. Betty had me take out a shirt for each of us on the trip and send the rest to Sharon. They can be sold to help raise funds.

Yesterday night we drove over to a farm and loaded many bales of hay into the rental truck. David and Betty had heard that hay in Alaska cost $15.00 a bale. They wanted to be sure that they had enough for their dogs' bedding. They also wanted to be sure that it was clean and fresh and insect free.

David and his friend, Rohn, are still working on the truck for the dogs. It will need to hold 20 full-grown mala-mutes.

After David and Rohn finish the dog truck, they will have to build a dog trailer. Someone was supposed to have done that for them already, but when he did not have not time to do it he simply brought the trailer back and dropped it off for them to do. That would not have been so bad except for the fact that he did it just a day or two ago. If he brought it back a month ago they would have had plenty of time to build the carrier onto it. Now they are really hard-pressed. Fortunately when Betty and David sold their old truck, they took the dog box off of it. David and Rohn plan to fasten it securely to the trailer. The box is made for 12 dogs. Since we have 32 to carry, it should work out just right.

The two men are working on it day and night. Meanwhile Betty continues to pack and takes care of the dogs.

I had a chance to get better acquainted with the dogs as Betty maintained their training and conditioning right up to the last minute before departure. A lot of hard work but it was def-initely a delightful task!

I was surprised when Betty opened the gate to a huge pen and released eight full grown young adult male malamutes. We strolled through the woods on an intentionally rough trail. At one point we were even pretty sure that we smelled a bear. As we traveled along the trail I was struck not only by the fact that this many males would run free together but by the happy friendly attitude of all of them. They would bound ahead and then return down the trail or out of the woods. They loved to be petted, patted and rubbed. In lieu of that they were also happy to stand on their hind legs and tap me playfully on top of the head. Actually that was Elim's specialty. He is irrepressible. His equally beautiful brother, Nicolai, had a gentler but equally friendly approach. The beautiful pair of Canadian brothers, Golovin and Rainy played happily also. I had trouble, then and for days, being able to tell Rainy from Grayling. And when it came to being difficult to tell apart, the nearly identical brothers, Alaska and Iditarod zoomed playfully in and out of the trees. Gateway was easy to identify as he oversaw all of them like a big brother (he is a few months older than most of the others).

When this marvelous group of fellows went back to their pen, we repeated the walk with a similar group of girls. I quickly learned to identify Brook, Galena and Kechikan but had a serious problem with the four gray girls that were so alike, even down to their markings, that I thought they were impossible to tell apart. Suntrana, Coleen, Delta, and Taylor are all distinct individuals each with her own personality, but even after a month of traveling with them I still need to really look, and look again, to see who I am talking to or petting.

As we strolled down the exercise trail the second time, I mentioned to Betty the brush piles that I had noticed on the first walk around. I wondered if they were kindling wood that hadn't been hauled in and chopped into fireplace lengths yet or if they were just tree trimmings that hadn't been burned yet. She told me they were neither. The first year they had the trail they found out that free-running malamutes enjoyed giving free rein to their own hunting instincts. No small things in the area were safe. If they were fast enough, squirrels were usually ok because of the many trees. Bunnies, mice, gophers and other ground dwellers were pretty much helpless victims without a refuge, so they cut small trees and brush out of the pathway and made piles at intervals so the little creatures would have a place to hide. It appeared to be working. The dogs sometimes gave a pile a sniff and a looking over, but they seemed to accept that they weren't allowed to dig into the piles to investigate further.

There were more than 30 dogs to be cared for. The residents of each pen were given a free run. The 13 acre compound was carefully planned to be complete with trails intentionally rough for training and conditioning of the whole dog as well as specifically for their feet, and a pond to acquaint them with warm weather water and cold weather ice and icy conditions. Then there was practice with training and commands. I have never enjoyed waiting to start a trip so much. I have also probably never tried to learn so much in so short a time.

Later that evening, I showed Betty the beginning of this trip journal. She liked the idea. I will be leaving some notebooks with David and Betty. I have asked them to write in the notebooks, a minimum three sentences per day. There is no maximum. We will see how it goes. It could be terrific. Time will tell.

Sunday December 9, 2001

The day was spent packing and exercising dogs again. It was wonderful to observe all of these beautiful animals running and romping together. At one point in the day I noticed Wolf, one of the older dogs, did not look quite right. When I mentioned this to Betty, she said she knew. She had been watching him closely lately. She had reason to believe he was having another round in his battle with cancer. She softly admitted that she expected it to be his last. Neither one of us could bring ourselves to talk about it any more than that.

I was able to run errands with Betty and we took several rolls of film to be processed. The men are still working feverishly getting the vehicles ready for the trip. We walked out in the evening and photographed them while they were welding. Betty talked a lot about the older dogs and their background. She also talked about their youngsters and their high hopes for them.

She told me about David thinking that Iditarod was too small to make the team. When they took him to an area weightpull he surprised David with his enthusiasm. In front of the training cart, he was an inspiration. Now he is one of the David's favorites.

She told me that later David was saying that perhaps Elim is too big. He said maybe we should sell him or find him a home. Maybe we should not take them with us to Alaska. She said "We have to take him with. I had a dream that he saved me from a bear." Elim was definitely going on this trip.

(Now, none of us claim to be superstitious, but I don't know of anybody who hasn't themselves or known somebody, who has known or felt something that cannot be explained.)

I realized then, and frequently throughout the trip that sometimes David played devil's advocate, weighing both sides of a question and often doing so verbally so as to get other people's input and opinions on the subject also.

One of the things that Betty was doing while we waited in the evenings was to work on harnesses. She had a big pile of them that looked new and freshly made. I know our mutual friend Delores had been working on making harnesses all summer for them. They appeared to be well-made and finished. Betty showed me what she was doing. She had a big spool of coarse thread, a big thick needle and a pair of pliers for push-

 ing the needle through the thick layers. With them she was sewing large round bells (like what used to be on horse harnesses in the winter time) onto the tops of the dog harnesses. I thought it was attractive and even "cutesy" for parades and public outings but wondered why she would be wasting time that was right now so valuable on something like that.

Betty explained to me that even to begin with they had not used the bells for appeal to humans. Although that was a sort of nice side effect when they were in parades and such, they used the bells to warn wildlife of the team's approach so they had time to get off of the trail before the dogs were upon them. (As one who has had her team consider anything smaller than a bus that happens to be on the trail to be fair game, I made a mental note to try to get some bells on my harnesses before next winter.) Now, Betty said, the bells might have an even more important use. In Alaska they might also serve to warn really big animals that they are coming. It might be her dogs that she is saving from harm if a bear or a moose hears the bells and avoids them. I'm all for that idea, too.

While I was in the kitchen with Betty, watching (helping?) her pack, David walked through and handed me a business card in an envelope. It is a card of Col. Norman Vaughan. I was impressed because I knew Col. Vaughan to be a dogsledding legend. When I turned the card over I was even more so. It contained a sort of thumbnail sketch of the highlights of the man's career. Wow! When I looked again at the face of the card I saw that Col. Vaughan had autographed it personally to David. That's when David told me that we were headed for

Trapper Creek, Alaska and the dog-handler's cabin behind that of Col. Vaughan. It seems that Norman Vaughan and David have struck up a friendship and Norman has encouraged David to follow the Britz's dream. He has been very supportive even to the point of renting them his extra cabin at a very reasonable rate. Ok, I'm impressed.

Later Betty tells me that the cabin is about 4 miles from the small town. She is really a people-person and enjoys visiting and doing many public contact and community service activities. She is concerned about being isolated. David is happy in the outdoors and doesn't seem to care as much about public contact. Oh yes, he does it and enjoys it too, but he doesn't seem to need people as much as she does. Only 4 miles out isn't bad though. Even if she doesn't use the truck, Betty can always just run the old team into town for a visit and a mail check while David is out on the trail training the young team.

It sounds Idyllic.

David says we will leave tonight but it is already very late and everyone is very tired.

Monday, December 10, 2001

I fell asleep last night in the middle of some of the boxes that were packed for the trip. I woke up with a blanket over me. Someone had covered me and put my feet up on the couch. When I looked around I discovered that David was packing the rental truck with equipment. Betty was finishing filling the last few boxes. Now we are really close to leaving.

Betty and I went over to Doug's house. David and Rohn had rearranged much of the equipment in the truck. We not only need to carry everything necessary, we have to be able to locate that which we will need along the way. Now the men were finishing with the arrangement of everything in the truck.

David had realized that we needed to finish some drop chains. They are the short chains that each individual dog is attached to the main chain picket line with. The brass snaps needed to be fastened securely to each end of the pre-cut short chains. Brass snaps are preferred because they don't freeze up even in the cold and snow. Because the dogs that we are dealing with are so powerful, and because they have never been tied out on a picket line (at least the young ones never have) we had to be sure that the drop chains would not fail. Therefore the links to fasten the chains to the snaps had to be very strong. We could not pinch them closed with simple hand tools. Doug has a very good bench vice in his workshop, so Doug and I worked together and finished the chains. I felt good to be able to contribute even that little bit.

One of the bits of chasing we can't do ahead of time with Betty's little car is to go get wood shavings. Once the dog truck is finished, David and Rohn take it to get some. When they come back they not only have bags of it for future use, they have poured an ample supply into each dog box for the comfort of every dog on the trip. Some of the chips are of aromatic red cedar. They smell nice and leave a nice aroma in the dogs' coats, but more important, they are said to be offensive to many parasites. Good. We don't want to be bringing any little tiny multi-legged hitch hikers with us.

Now it is getting dark and we are almost ready to go. We are finally ready. The last things that we must put into the truck are the dogs. The plan that we have is for me to record this activity with a video camera, so I will stop writing for now.

Later...Maybe.. Monday December 10, or maybe.. very early Tuesday, December 11.

My, my, my... preparing and actually getting onto the road was quite an experience in itself. Due to the many delays, the dog truck was newly finished. The young team had never been taught to ride in or even to get into this dog truck or anything like it.

It was dark by the time we were ready to go. We decided to load the dogs by the porch light. The plan was for me to videotape the start of this great expedition. Betty walked out to release the dogs one pen at a time. They could run down to

David. He would then load them into the truck. I sat down on the porch steps to record this for posterity.

All went well as the old freight team galloped cheerfully down to David. With his help they climbed into their familiar boxes on the dog trailer and settled down contentedly waiting for a ride.

Then the youngsters! I sat on the porch steps with my elbows braced on my knees for a nice stable shot of the action... yeah... right! Out of the darkness charged the herd that I had first walked the trail with. They gleefully romped to David, then around him, then on to inspect the large strange lump on the porch steps. If you think that it is difficult to walk and/or take snapshots with large friendly dogs jumping all over, you should try to film while being trapped in a highly animated cross-cuddle.

When things, mostly the big fellows, calmed down a bit David started to load the dogs. I have always suspected... and now I'm sure it is true... that one of the reasons that racers run those little 35- pound Alaskans is because they are easy to pick up and toss into the dog truck. If I ever doubted it, the site of David with a 90# malamute wrapped around his head as he

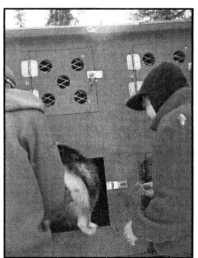

tried to stuff it into one of those little doors would convince me. To make the project more interesting was the fact that these robust youngsters had never been in a dog truck. Imagine trying to stuff these big puppies in while they have a paw on each side of the door, looking in and the debating if they really want to do this. I don't need to imagine it. I saw it many times last night. What a job!

We finally had everybody and everything loaded and ready. I'm afraid I must admit that it has been years since I started a trip with a prayer. When David suggested it, it felt right! As we stood hand in hand asking for help and guidance I realized the quiet and powerful depth of Betty and David's faith. This was the first official prayer on this trip, but believe me, it wasn't the last unofficial one!

I climbed into the equipment truck, (which I was to drive every foot of the way to Alaska). David and Betty rode the dog

truck. We picked up Doug and headed out. I was a little concerned about this 80 year-old man as both Betty and David sort of shoved and lifted to get him up into the high cab of the rental truck.

It was really very late to be starting such a long journey but our need to actually get going was overpowering. When that time had finally come, it was necessary to hit the road. After the days of preparation everybody was very tired. We only drove a few hours. One of our main concerns was the question whether or not the tightly packed equipment truck was over its allowed weight. We have stopped in a parking lot to discuss this possibility and to take a reasonably short nap. If the truck scales at the state line close by the time we get there.... oh well.

Even later that night....

We have crossed the first two state lines, traveling through the upper corner of Wisconsin, and then into Minnesota. As we crossed a huge high bridge at Duluth, it occurred to me that I had failed to mention to David anything about my phobia of bridges. As I followed the dog truck I decided to give David a hard time about it.

We found a truck stop with a scale. Wow! Are we over!

A truck driver from Canada was discussing the route with David. He suggested that we just telephone the Minnesota department of transportation and get overweight permits. These are much much cheaper than fines. It sounds like a good idea to me. David says he will call them in the morning. Right now we are sitting at the far edge of a parking lot outside of a casino.

Tuesday, December 11, 2001

After a few hours of sleep, we awakened in the parking lot of this large casino in Minnesota. The first thing that we needed to do was to "drop the dogs". This was going to be our way of life for the next few weeks.

We had about a dozen dogs tied out on the chains. Several people stopped to admire them. David and Betty were happy to tell people about their dogs and their hopes and their goal for this adventure. One very pleasant couple listened with great interest and really seemed to admire not only the dogs but also the brave young people with the great aspirations. They offered to buy all of us breakfast at the casino coffee shop. We were not even half of the way through taking care of the dogs. There was no way either David or Betty would consider stopping or even taking a break before every dog was cared for. They very politely explained this to these friendly people. The strangers were very pleasant and understanding. They said that the offer still stood. If we wanted to join them, they would wait for us inside the coffee shop. They accepted the fact that it would probably be more than an hour wait. Under those circumstances Betty and David agreed to come

and meet them inside when we were finished.

It took a long time, but finally all of the dogs were cared for and back in the dog truck. We were all quite happy to go into a warm cheerful coffee shop and enjoy a very tasty meal and some excellent company. Flo and Ernie Strandberg of nearby Carlton, Minnesota, were very interesting and charming people. This was our first experience with a totally spontaneous act of kindness from people wishing us well and contributing materially and with wonderful encouragement to this whole project. We hated to leave them but we had to get back on the road.

When we were ready to go again, David called the Minnesota department of transportation. He came back over to the trucks looking very upset. The official that he had spoken with said to him that they would issue no overload permit. We should just continue on our way. When they stopped us at the state line they would confiscate all of the overweight in dog food. We would have no choice in the matter.

Poor David had worked himself all weekend to his physical limit just getting everything finished and on the road. Betty was pretty much in the same shape. It had been a monumental task to try to pack everything they might need. Especially because they weren't sure if they were going for five months or for two years or any time in between. The last day they also to had to close down their house for whatever time it might be. Now they were in danger of losing a vital amount of their provisions. It was a serious blow. We got on the road and started driving. Then we pulled over to talk about our options. At first it didn't seem like we had any. We thought perhaps the answer would be to lighten the load before we got to the scales. Yes, that sounded like a good plan. The next question was how to do it. We thought of jettisoning some of the straw.... but where? What would we do with it? Dumping it would be a financial loss. How to get rid of it was a problem in itself. We couldn't just dump a ton or so of straw by the side of the road. We drove on. We were traveling through woodlands and farm country. Farm country? Farmers not only make straw, they also use it. If we could find someone to buy it even at a reduced price at least it wouldn't be a total loss. The next question, of course, was where to find someone to buy it. How about a farmer's co-op? The next town along the way was Wright, Minnesota. The co-op was easy to find.

I went into the place with David. (Because he was one and will probably be one again sometimes, David knows how to talk to truck drivers. Me, I speak fluent farmer with a minor in co-op. I have also come to realize that men ask questions to get answers. Women ask questions to solve problems. I know that sounds sexist but I consider it merely an observation.) David asked the woman in charge if the co-op bought and sold straw. Did they want to buy some from us? When the answer was no, David turned to leave hoping to find somewhere else further on. I quickly explained the situation and included the information about what good people I was traveling with. Jill and Bev really tried to come through for us. They made telephone calls to several places to see if anyone wanted to buy our straw. When they could find no one, they allowed David to use their telephone to contact a friend of his near St. Paul. We could store some things with him, but driving it down there would cost us six hours of time and many miles. While David was on the phone the folks from the co-op were also trying to come up with a way to help. They offered David storage space. He could leave some heavy things there and send for them later. While David and Betty worked with a co-op employee selecting and unloading, I got to show off the dogs and the dog truck to people at the co-op. We left about 4000

lbs. in one of their storage barns. I just can't say enough about how nice these strangers were to us.

Continuing, we went to a truck stop and re-weighed both trucks. We found that we could take some of the weight off of the dog trailer and put it in the big truck. This would save wear and tear on both the trailer and the dog truck. When we were making the change over, David and Betty discussed the stress on the trailer tires. They also talked about the fact that it was getting late in the afternoon and the dogs had not been out of their boxes since early morning. They decided that when we got to Brainerd, Minnesota, we would install trailer tires and drop dogs. So that is what we did.

We stopped at a farm and truck supply chain store. We set up and dropped the dogs at the outer edge of the parking lot. There was a gas station not too far away where we could get water for the dogs. While the dogs relaxed and had their dinner, David was hard at work purchasing and then changing tires.

We, or rather the dogs, began to attract attention. People would drive past and then slow down and turn into the parking lot to get a closer look. After this happened several times, we invited a man with a little girl to get out and pet the dogs. We knew that the dogs would like it as much as the child. Once we had broken the ice, we had many people bringing their children over to see these giant animated teddy bears. They were all considerate enough to ask for permission before they approached the malamutes. Of course permission was always granted. As tired as everybody was, this began to feel almost like a children's party. Adults as well as children appeared to really enjoy these furry good will ambassadors. As this was going on the big store behind us closed. It was getting late. Our visitors thinned out as people took their children home to bed. One woman approached Betty before she left. She told her how wonderful the dogs looked and shook her hand. As the woman walked away, Betty looked down to see money in her own hand. When she told me about it later her eyes were glistening. She was so touched by this unsolicited kindness and encouragement.

Once the dogs are back in their boxes we make sure all organic matter from the dogs is collected and properly disposed of in a dumpster, with the permission of the dumpster's owner. Then to my surprise, they go back over the whole area with a wide shovel and scrape up even the little bit of wood chips that have spilled onto the ground when the dogs got out of their boxes.

We sleep for awhile in the parking lot, and then get back under way.

Wednesday, December 12, 2001

When it was clear daylight, we pulled into a truck stop to drop the dogs. During that process, Betty decided that this would be a good time to label each dog's box. We took a magic marker and wrote each name below the correct door. It was fun to do and it was good practice to help me remember their names. I found myself wishing that I could purchase a small can of golden paint. The temperature was well below freezing so I couldn't do it that way anyhow. By the time we finished labeling the 20 boxes in the brand new dog truck, the cold was getting to my hands. The names were not very straight and the lettering was less than perfect. David and Betty generously and genuinely seemed to be quite pleased with it. I think they are just pleased to see their dogs names in writing. It is almost like the truck now belongs to their dogs. I watch them as they handle the dogs. It is more than just good care and proper treatment. They handle them... they touch them with love and affection. Even when David is trying to stuff big dogs through small doors as high as his head, through the puffing and grunt-

ing, with Betty trying to slide paws off the sides and into the openings, they are talking encouragingly to the dogs. Whenever I look at either of them while they are looking at their dogs I see a softness in their expressions. Betty always refers to the dogs as their "fur children". This is not just a figure of speech to them. To try to describe it any further I would have to wax so corny that it would be intolerable even to me. I'm sure the two of them don't see me making this observation. In fact I think they are totally unaware of the almost childlike love that shows on their faces at such times.

After the hours it took to care for the dogs, we went into the restaurant for a warm meal. While we were in there, David, as usual, talked to truckers and other people there. Several of them mentioned that we should expect a hard time crossing the border. Everybody trying to cross with a box truck like the one I was driving, was getting stopped and told to unload it for inspection. This was not the first time that we had heard this.

One of the people talking to David suggested a short route that would take us to Winnepeg, Manitoba. Our original plan was to stay in the United States and travel west across the northern tier of states. We had not planned to cross the border until we were at the Rocky Mountains, but we were in desperate need of something to lift our spirits. By now we felt that we had been running in place and just wanted to get out of Minnesota. The people we had met had been just wonderful but we really shared the feeling that we had been there too long and wanted to be on our way. We took the man's advice and headed north.

We gassed up the trucks in Bemidji, Minnesota. As we drove out of the station I looked at the numbers on the pump. Somehow it doesn't seem right that David would put 71 gallons of diesel fuel into the 50 gallon tank on this truck. Since David was driving out ahead of me, I had no choice but to follow. I will tell him about it later but of course by then it will be too late to do anything about it. I wonder how many people that happens to and how long that particular station will get away with it.

It was still a long drive. We needed to make one more improvement. The necessity of carrying dogs in a trailer did not sit too well with any of us, but even with special mirrors, neither Betty nor David could see the trailer behind them. We finally stopped at a service station and convenience store and bought the kind of reflectors that people put at the end of their driveways. We stood out in the snow in the gathering dusk, taping the long legs of these things to the framework of the trailer. At least they could be seen from inside the dog truck. Betty said she felt a little bit better to have some visual contact with "her babies". We continued north.

Canada

Wednesday December 12, 2001
Late at night.

We made it! We finally made it! We are finally out of Minnesota! The best part of it is the fact that we finally made it into Canada!

For awhile I think that we all thought that we were never going to get here. We did better than we expected. I think at every truckstop we heard tales of how difficult it was to cross the border. The very large box truck that I was driving would make matters even more complicated, is what we were told. Everyone that tried to cross the border with such a truck was pulled over to the side and told they had to completely unload it for inspection. We approached the border crossing at about 10:00 in the evening. If we had to unload, it would take us until dawn to do it. Then it would probably take all morning to reload. We were not looking forward to it but were prepared to do it if necessary.

I am sure that vigilance has increased hundreds of percent since September 11. Good thing too. We would rather that there were too much security than not enough. We weren't real eager for the extra work, however.

Besides the box truck, we had many other special considerations. Obviously, first and foremost, were the dogs. They needed to be properly identified and have all of their health and vaccinations up-to-date. All of this needed to be verified on paper. Another big consideration was the fact that we were trying to cross the border with guns in our possession. David and Betty had decided to bring along a shotgun and David's military rifle. Living and sledding out in the wilds of Alaska might make them necessary for protection, even survival. Yes, we were approaching the border checkpoint with many cards stacked against us.

The border guard said that Doug and I should remain in the truck. We should not get out unless we were told to. We knew that we would need our papers in order also.

While we were waiting we took them out. Douglas Johnson had his birth certificate. It was issued from Atlantic Mill, Michigan. Interestingly enough though, it was written in Finnish. We were a little bit concerned, but it was obviously from Michigan. I had my passport in my pocket but all the border guard asked for was my driver's license. When I pulled it out I accidentally-on-purpose left my badge lying on the dash board. Sometimes a little professional courtesy goes a long way. I need not have bothered.

Betty had been working on this part of the project for a long time. She had made many calls to the Canadian government to be sure of what was needed. She had all the paperwork for the dogs and for the guns in perfect order. The border guard made a few telephone calls apparently to verify which information was necessary. He looked at the paperwork, checked the dog truck and trailer, and walked to the back of our truck. He and David opened the doors and gave it a good look with his flashlight. He came to my window and asked for the paper work from Douglas and myself. It appeared to satisfy him. I am sure that he was impressed with Betty's mastery of all the necessary papers.

Then to my surprise he waved us on through. From the time we pulled in to the time we pulled out, it was only about one half-hour.

Hooray ! We are in Canada.

We drove on to Winnipeg, Manitoba.

We found a truck stop and dropped the dogs. Betty noticed that Wolf appears to be feeling a lot better today. Tundra however seems to be slowing down. This worries Betty because he is sixteen years old.

I finally called home again. I have been putting it off because I didn't want them to know how close to home we still were. When they asked me where I was I said, "Somewhere between the Minnesota and Alaska state lines." Mom's OK. She says Lori took Lily to the veterinarian. Lily should deliver soon. Probably four or five puppies. I sure want to get back home in time for that.

Mom also said that Nicole telephoned from Belgium. I sure hate to miss her calls. They are always so interesting. I think I will wait a few days and call her back from Alaska.

Thursday, December 13, 2001

It was cold last night and it's cold this morning. We dropped the dogs at the break of dawn. While we had one group of them out, a man came over and admired them. He said his name was Joseph. Of course we allowed him to meet and touch them. He seemed quite comfortable, even familiar with them. No wonder. He was used to malamutes. His wife is a breeder in Ontario. He wished us well and walked away as we continued with morning chores.

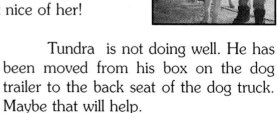

Very soon he came back. He was speaking on his cell phone. He handed the telephone to me. His wife, Brigitte Wiatowski, of Mimmenuk Kennels was on the phone to greet us and to send well wishes to Betty and David. She informs us that information about the trip is on the Internet. Wasn't that nice of her!

Tundra is not doing well. He has been moved from his box on the dog trailer to the back seat of the dog truck. Maybe that will help.

Betty emerges from the back of the dog truck carrying a huge plastic bag. She opens it. It is filled with bright stuffed toys. She walks from door to door in the

67

dog truck and gives a soft fluffy new toy to each inhabitant. Tundra gets his in the back seat also.

We drive out and head west. A little way from the city of Winnipeg, Manitoba, we picked up Canadian Highway Number One. We follow that west past Portage la Prairie, Manitoba, then pick up Canadian Highway 16. This highway is known as the Yellowhead Route. Now we are traveling slightly north and very west.

I picked up the truck one week ago today. According to our original plan we were supposed to get on the road right away. Allowing six days for travel we should have been approaching the Alaskan state line by now. Boy! Are we far off! It's a good thing that we are flexible.

As we are driving Doug mentions that there are no guard rails along the highway. I really think nothing of it. A few hours later he mentions it again. At first I am puzzled, then I realize that he worked for his county's highway department for 30 years or so. He is making a professional observation.

We continue driving and cross our first Province line. We have entered Saskatchewan. We drive as far as Yorkton, Saskatchewan, where we find a truck stop and drop the dogs again. It is very cold. I help a little bit and then join Doug inside the restaurant.

I never would have believed that I would shower in a truckstop, but I did and it felt great! I feel so refreshed. I put on my dream team T-shirt. I can't believe a couple of dollars can make a person feels so good. David and Betty will get their showers in the morning. We can all use the lift.

When David and Betty finally come in they look unhappy, Wolf is not doing well. His breath is cold. Betty tells me that is how another one of her dogs was just before it passed away. Now I am worried too. There is nothing any of us can do about it.

Friday, December 14, 2001

Dateline Saskatchewan. I am sitting in the truck thawing my fingers and watching David and Betty out caring for the dogs as the sun rises behind them. I make a few brief notes and then head into the building to join Doug waiting for them.

Later I walk from the restaurant over to the truckers area to see if the showers are empty. As I walk past the entry, David and Betty come through the doors. Her face is turned down and hidden. David's face looks pinched. It is more than just being tired. I try to look into his blue eyes. They are wet. He says softly, "Wolf is dead."

The three of us put our arms around each other and stand there crying ..... in the lobby of a truckstop ... in a strange country... we don't care.. it doesn't matter.

We drive all day and get to Lloydminster. The Province-line between Saskatchewan and Alberta runs right through Lloydminster. We pull into a truck stop on the Alberta side of town. I telephone home when I go in for water. David and Betty are still setting up the chains. I will be back before they have the dogs out. Lily is in the process of the delivering. Four puppies so far.

When the dogs are finished, we go back inside for supper. I phone home again. The total is five healthy little puppies. I am pleased. David and Betty congratulate me. They are genuinely happy for me. I am so grateful that Lori and Delores were there for me and for my little Lily. I know they are fine and in very competent hands. But I am so unhappy at missing this blessed event that I fail to see the irony in this day.

Saturday, December 15, 2001

On the road again. We are having problems with this rental truck. The engine light came on and stayed on. The road seems as flat as a pancake. There may be a gradual steady climb but it really doesn't look like it. The light stayed on until we stopped, and I turned off the engine. When I restarted, the light was off.

We have also discovered that the windshield washers do not work. Last night while we were driving, Betty was riding with me. The windows kept getting dirty. We had trouble seeing the road. Sometimes we stopped and threw our drinking water on the windshield, and then turned on the wipers. Once, Betty tried to open the hood to see if she could clear any blockage. Another truck went by and the wind it created threw the hood out of Betty 's hand. For one instant she was snapped like a rag doll and almost thrown into traffic. We both got frightened. I insisted that Betty get back in the truck. She was so shook up that she obeyed. After that we would just fill our soda pop bottles with water and reach our hands out of the side windows of the truck to squirt the windshield.

Driving down the road on the way to Edmonton, Alberta, the window keeps getting mud thrown from the road by other vehicles. The windshield wipers can only push so much of it aside. The engine light comes back on. With more mud on the windshield I can barely see out as traffic becomes thick and more constant the closer we get to the city. I drive into Edmonton virtually blind.... and angry.

We are all also very unhappy with the tires on this truck. They are certainly not snow tires. They are very smooth, really for summer driving. They are definitely not the kind of tires anyone would want to drive with in the winter time. Absolutely not for driving through the mountains. David has declared that we will look to see if this rental truck chain had a franchise in Edmonton. We stop for fuel and the people in the office of this station are very helpful. We locate the truck company office in their phone book and they tell us how to get there.

When we drive into the rental company's lot, a man comes out to offer assistance. One look at the truck and he says it's not one of theirs. We insist that it is. The name of the company in letters over 2 ft.tall on the side of the truck certainly lends credence to our claim. We explain our major problems to him. We don't even mention the bent step or the door that doesn't close properly on the passenger side or the fact that the headlights are pointing anywhere but at the road...no matter how often we adjust them. All we are asking to be repaired are issues of safety not convenience. He does something to the windshield washer line as he is explaining to us they must have authorization to work on this truck. He still doesn't believe it is one of theirs. He asks us for the registration to verify. We look in all the pouches, pockets and shelves. There is no registration to be found. I am dumbfounded. How could I be so foolish? I certainly should have realized that before now. We show them the rental contract. He is still doubtful, but tries to call the office we got the truck from.

The next hour or two will always remain in my head sort of as a surrealistic movie. This poor man telephoned place after place. He went to the truck several times for information. He tried calling local and national offices in the United States and Canada. At one point, during all the telephone and delay, Betty turned to me and said,"This is happening for a reason." I knew just what she meant but I couldn't explain it either.

At the end of all of this several "facts" came to light. First of all, the truck I was driving was supposed to be strictly a day rental truck, not for over-the-road at all. It is supposed to be illegal to rent it out as such. There was no registration form anywhere in the truck. This is another thing that is illegal. There were several mixed up messages from various offices. Some said we did not actually have a company truck, but one that had been sold but the name had not been painted off. Some said we weren't supposed to have crossed the border. We were driving illegally. Some said we and the truck didn't exist at all.

It seems that the only thing they agreed on was that we had no over-the-road protection. The entire answer to us was, "You're on your own."

The whole experience is upsetting. We leave Edmonton troubled and angry. Angry with the United States offices of that company, not with the Canadian branch. The people there have been very good to us. They have tried their best to be helpful. We ruefully tell ourselves that at least we have the windshield washers working.

We continue on our journey. Douglas and I in the equipment truck as usual are following the dog truck. A little way down the road, Doug calls my attention to a problem. The rear lights on the dog truck are dark. They are running lights. They should be on all the time the truck is on the road. We manage to flag David down and tell him. He tries hard but can't locate the problem. The headlights and emergency flashers work however, so we decide to try to limp to the next major town. As we continue the windshield washers on the big truck stop working. Betty says, "This is happening for a reason." Now I am really beginning to feel uncomfortable.

We have turned off the Yellowhead highway. It started angling more to the south. We are heading a strong northwest. As darkness begins to gather around us, we are trying to get to a reasonably large community. David pulls over and walks back to talk to us. He says that Betty wants to pull over somewhere for the night. I suggest going as far as Whitecourt. It is only 20 or 30 miles ahead. David returns to the dog truck and we continue.

We see a sign for a little town just off the highway. Not 2 miles further David pulls into a parking lot. The building there is occupied by a Chinese restaurant in one half and what appears to be a service station in the other half. He is almost apologetic as he comes over. He explains that Betty insisted that we get off the road. She is in tears. I have no problem with listening to her feelings. Now the only problem is just what we will do. The man in the station is not too sure that he wants us to drop the dogs in his lot. He says we should get permission from the restaurant also. Actually the lighting is not very good and it looks like we would have trouble getting water for the dogs. It is still a little early so we decide to go into the restaurant for a hot meal and to talk over the situation.

When we get inside I ask the waitress if there's a motel nearby. Up until now we had been sleeping in the trucks. We had all started this trip tired and stressed out. Now we need some place with a large parking lot, good lighting and some access to water. Maybe a night's sleep where we could lie down and straighten out our legs would be a big help.

Before we even get seated at a table, the waitress has the local motel on the telephone for me. I explain our situation to the man on the other end of the line. I make sure to tell him exactly how considerate David and Betty really are. He tells me that it is the motel's policy to not accept guests with dogs. Then with no hesitation he goes on to say that he believes me and we would be welcome to stay there. I get directions to the place and then we all sit down to a warming relaxing meal.

If the stop in Edmonton was like a surrealistic movie....our stay in Sandugo is more like a Disney one.

We drive back to where we saw the turnoff for that town just off the highway. The name of the place is Sandugo. We follow the directions to the motel. We drive down a little hill and stop both trucks between high snow banks. We go into the office and identify ourselves. Ken and Sharon of the Arcadian Motel greet us warmly and instruct us to go to the parking lot behind the motel. Our room is back there and we will have sufficient space to drop the dogs. Their only request is that we don't tie them so close to the building that they can make markings on the guests' doors.

When we get back there we discover a huge area. We can set up the chains at least 50 feet from the doors. There is no one else in this lot. We position the trucks about 30 or 40 feet apart and stretch the chains between them. Getting water is no problem. We just go into our motel room and fill our big water jugs in the bathtub.

The room we are assigned is wonderful. It is more like a suite or a self-contained cabin. When you enter the first room, there is a bed and a couch-bed. Turn to the left and pass a large bedroom with a chair, a dresser and a huge double bed.

Ahead is a huge bathroom containing fresh fluffy towels and, best of all, hot water. If you go back the way you came, behind the first room there is a dining area and a small kitchen. Not really all that small and stocked with dishes and pots and pans... even a toaster. Not only a stove and refrigerator, there is a working coffee pot and a supply of coffee and tea.

Before we even arrived, we were feeling that we were welcome. The warmth with which we were greeted, deepened that feeling. Once we had the chains out and were putting the dogs on them, people came to see the malamutes. A friend of Ken and Sharon's and her child came first. Beautiful Aurora made sure to show the little child that an Alaskan Malamute is really just an animated Teddy bear. Ken had called his brother and the two of them came out to visit. They seemed to like all the dogs but sweet little Kechi really appeared to charm them. We took pictures of all of them with the dogs. It is hard to tell who had the most fun... the people enjoying seeing these big friendly dogs, or the malamutes enjoying being admired and petted. With the convenience of nearby water and that huge area we were allowed to use, the dog care appeared to go more smoothly than usual. After hot showers, the clean sheets were just wonderful! We all appreciated a good night's sleep.

Sunday, December 16,2001

In the morning we all felt better. While the dogs were out for their morning break David and Doug worked on the truck light problem. When they needed parts Ken found a place to get them. The men discussed the fact that the big truck had only one fuel tank. This was another one of the concerns that we didn't get to address back in Edmonton. Ken generously located someone with a steel 55-gallon drum. He took David to get it in his own truck. That way the dogs could remain tied out between our two trucks. Ken even had someone to fill the drum with diesel fuel. He managed all of this help on a Sunday morning. Once the full fuel drum was safely installed in the back cargo area of the big truck, the men realized that it was a long way from the fuel tank that actually fed the engine. That was located just under the passenger door of the cab of the truck. If we ran low on fuel, how would we refill the main tank? Ken had a solution. He unselfishly gave us his own garden hose. David carried it into the bathroom of our suite and hung it on the shower rod to thaw out and drain.

While they were working on that problem, Betty continued taking care of the dogs. Tundra seems to have perked up. His appetite has returned. He is even moving around better. Baby Kotzebue keeps herself and any dog near her entertained bouncing and running around within the confines of the 6 foot circle her chain allows her. With the same happy-go-lucky attitude several of the young dogs play together on the picket line. Even the older team seems to be enjoying the extra time out. Some play with the youngsters and some of them just bask in the sun. There appears to be a contented look about them as they stretch out on top of the snow.

Meanwhile back at our room... There was a knock on the door. Sharon brought some things over from her own kitchen. Apparently while she was talking to Betty, she found out that David had asked someone at the restaurant the night before if there was a grocery store nearby. They had planned to stock up our supply for further travel. Whoever they asked had told them no. Sharon was upset. There was a grocery store right in town. It would have still been open when we got there last night. She was concerned that we would have to go on our way without even getting breakfast. She was not about to let that happen. She had come with her arms full of food from her own home. She handed us eggs and bacon and bread and butter....even milk for our coffee or tea. We could make breakfast in the convenient kitchen. With the coffee we already had brewing it was a veritable feast.

When Betty came back in I told her what Sharon had done. She was surprised and deeply touched but also enthused about the prospect of such a nice meal before we got on the road. Then she informed me that the men had gone out for some supplies and she was not sure when they would be back.

We decided not to cook the eggs right away. Everybody knows how ickey cold eggs are. The bacon we could start now. As I reached for the toaster, I had another thought. If we scrambled the eggs with a little bit of milk, we could make French toast. We could keep that warm in the oven so it was ready when the fellows came back. As I was doing that, Sharon came back to tell us that the guys had gone. When she saw me making French toast, she commented that she had not thought of that. We did not have any syrup. She was gone almost before we realized it. She reappeared carrying a bottle of that delicious sweet stuff. None of us (then or even now) would get over how thoughtful and considerate this woman and her husband were toward complete strangers.

When the men came back we had a lovely big breakfast. While we all enjoyed it immensely, David really dug into his sweet syrupy stack! I think that was when I realized that eating was one of David's favorite pastimes. I teased him about it. That didn't phase him one bit. In fact as we talked we discovered that David was down in weight and needed to put on a few pounds. (This became a subject of good natured kidding for the rest of this trip.) When we were children we used to say that someone like that had a hollow leg. It

appears that he can eat and eat and not really gain weight. Lucky guy.

Ken and Sharon had been so wonderful to us that we hated to leave. But we needed to finish our journey. So we packed up and headed out.

On to the highway to continue our travel. As we drive along we observe many tracks in the snow alongside the roadway. Even though the snow must be 3-6 ft. deep, I have never seen so many animal tracks. They come out of the woods, running uphill or down, and cross the highway in dozens... perhaps hundreds of places. There is one spot where a large area of snow is disturbed. It looks like a large vehicle might possibly have run off the road there. As I am wondering about it, Betty is making the same observations and wondering, ahead in the other truck. We will never know what we avoided, if anything, by getting off the road last night. Nevertheless, we were glad that we did.

The rolling hills have given way to some pretty serious climbs and drops. The truck I am driving is having serious problems dealing with the road conditions. It cannot handle steep climbs without some steady downshifting. The highways have not had the snow plowed off of them all the way down to the pavement since we entered Alberta. The lack of traction with these summer tires was one of the main reasons that we had looked for help back in Edmonton. Now the snow on the road combined with the sharp ups and downs causes the rubber to leave the road if we try to go very fast. Unfortunately, what the truck considers fast is way below the speed limit.

While we were eating this morning, we could talk more calmly and more rationally about the situation with the rental truck. We are pretty sure we have been scammed from the start. That was probably the cause of the big foul up in the beginning. We have decided that Betty and David will telephone the bank in the morning and put a hold on any payment that company tries to collect.

Because of our late beginning and the slow pace of the

truck, we only drive as far Grande Prairie. We are spending a third night in the province of Alberta. It is a good thing that the people here are so wonderful. However, we feel that we need to show some progress and cross another line very soon.

Dropping the Dogs

I think that this is a good time to stop and clarify a term that I have been using throughout this journal. The term... "Dropping the Dogs." It is a very simplified phrase to label a very extensive process. I will try to explain our routine.

✖ The first step is to select a location. This is actually more of a challenge than one might think. There has to be sufficient room to allow us to park the trucks 30 or 40 ft. apart. This has to be enough out of traffic that we can spread the dogs out between the trucks and still be able to walk all around our area and freely move people, equipment and dogs in and out of the trucks and around the entire tie out area. Not only did we have to think of the size of the parking area we needed, we also required sufficient lighting to see what we were doing and move freely. We also had to have someplace nearby with virtually unlimited access to water. It takes many gallons of it to keep more than 30 large dogs from dehydrating. We learned along the way that we also had to pay attention to which direction the wind was coming from.

Early in the trip we found that we needed to start the trucks and run them several times during the night. This was a requirement for two reasons. First of all we needed to make use of the heaters for our own comfort. More importantly, however, we needed to be sure that the trucks would restart in the cold weather. Later in the trip we found it necessary to just to let the trucks (at least the rental) run all night at idle speed. Since we had to run the trucks, we had to be very conscious of exactly where the exhaust fumes were going. The dogs in their boxes would be very vulnerable to it.

✖ Once we selected an ideal location there was still the

78

matter of getting permission to use it. We usually stopped at truck stops with huge parking lots. If they were open all night for us to get water, that usually took care of the problem. But sometimes the buildings were closed, and sometimes there was no truck stop available so we had to find another parking lot of sufficient size. It was for these variations that permission was sometimes a problem. If we were denied, we would have to continue driving until we found a location that we could use.

✖ Once we had located where we were going to drop the dogs, we needed to arrange the trucks in a functional manner. The next step was to set up the chains. First David had to get them out of the back of the big truck. He carried the heavy chains in large buckets. I personally could not lift one of them. The long chains were then strung from the front tires of one truck to those of the other truck. To keep them from damaging either truck that chains were wrapped around the tires while lying on the ground. Each chain was fastened to itself. The loop of chain could certainly not be pulled out from under the tires of the heavy the trucks. This was done from each side of the trucks so the result was two long parallel lines of picket chains. The short drop chains were attached to them at intervals.

✖ We were then finally able to actually take the dogs out of their boxes on the truck and trailer. This was more of a production than one might think.

✖ The first step was to take the padlocks off the long steel rods that had been slid through holders the entire length of the body of the dog box. They were there to keep the individual doors from opening. That way no stranger would have access to any individual dog while we were not looking. There was a locking steel rod for each line of dog doors. That meant four of them on the truck and four of them on the dog box in the trailer.

Once each of the rods had been slid carefully free of the holders and stored on the trailer, individual dog doors could be unlocked and each turnbuckle opened. Only then the dogs, one at a time, could be taken out and put on the picket line.

Each drop chain was about 3 ft. long. That meant a 6 foot circle that each individual dog had available to trot around. They were set so that each one of them could touch the dog next to it but the chains would not quite overlap. That way they could play together but they would not get tangled up. This was a consideration taking into account the parallel chains also. Every dog had at least one companion to play with while out on the chains. That way getting out of the truck not only meant that they could relieve themselves but also that it was play time. This was physically very beneficial. The puppies could play together and the older dogs would get much needed incentive to move about and increase circulation and muscular exercise. It was also very important to keep all of them well socialized with one another. Romping together was also good for their morale. Seeing them happy and playing was good for our morale too.

✖ Once enough dogs were out of the truck, care for them began. Somebody would go and fill up the two 5 gal. water jugs (for the first of many times). David needed to go into the truck and bring out their various forms of dog food. Almost every day they needed to open a bag of the prepared kibble. With that they mixed other ingredients to create the balance of nutrition that was required for that meal. They usually added cut up pieces of meat and or fat. After that Betty or David walked around with a huge jar of a good quality vitamin mineral supplement making sure each dog received his or her requirements. The food had water mixed into it before it was served to the dogs. After the meal each dog also received a bowl of water.

✖ As things appeared naturally on the surface of the snow from the dogs relieving themselves (yellow stains or steaming piles) they were immediately cleaned up so no one had a chance of getting dirty by it and so it didn't get scattered around and overlooked. It was also an important part of care to check this material for any indications of problems, illness, or gastric upset so they could be dealt with immediately.

✖ When all of the dogs were full and comfortable most of them were allowed to play with each other while Betty and David each took one off the picket line and placed it on a long leash. Then they would take off and run around with the dog. They would usually run about 40 or 50 yards up and back and allow the canine to run in big circles around them at the end of a ten or fifteen foot leash. After a few laps up and down they would put that dog back on the picket line and repeat the performance with another individual. Betty and David did this until every dog had had a run. As they took the dogs out of the truck they checked them for condition, weight, and to be sure they had not injured themselves or gotten sores while riding in the box. They watched the dogs moving while on the picket line as they fed them, and again while they were running them all around. When everybody had been tended to this way it was time to put them back into their own boxes. That, of course, was a whole project in itself, but since I have already covered it in this book I won't go back into it except to say that by the very end of the trip the youngsters did learn to be a little more cooperative... but David swears that not one of them felt like he or she had lost one ounce of weight. He also vowed to

make a ramp for the dogs to load themselves just as soon as he had the time.

✖ Because of the spacing needed to allow the dogs to move around it was only possible to do ten to fifteen dogs at a time. That meant that the process, everything from taking the dogs out of their boxes to returning them at the end, had to be repeated two or three times every time we dropped dogs.   Doug usually helped by walking Dehlia and sometimes Tundra also.

(I grew to be a great disappointment to myself because as the trip wore on I found myself having more and more trouble with my hands and was less and less help in the actual job of dog care. I was never actually cold. I wore a warm hat and a double insulated flannel shirt as a jacket. I carried along a big 'for dogsledding' coat but never used it outside on the way up to Alaska. However, my hands would react to the cold with pain and severe weakness. I always wound up climbing back into the warm truck after a very short time. I could make sandwiches and keep notes in my journal. Sometimes I would take or try to take pictures, or videotape the activity of the others through the truck windows. Very disheartening. No one ever said anything at all bad about that which was was troubling me so much. In fact a few times that Betty saw me struggling she told me to get into the warm truck.)

✖ When every dog had been cared for and was safely back in its own box for the night (or for the day's travel) each dog door was individually locked and the long steel rods were

slid back into place. If we didn't move the trucks and if we had parked properly according to the wind direction, the big truck was no threat to the dogs. David would then take some long tubes, about 4 inches in diameter and 6-8 feet long, and place them over the tail pipe of the dog truck. He would then brace them to keep them from blowing away by shoveling snow

onto and around them. This was to divert the exhaust fumes from that truck from coming too close to the dog boxes. He would then join Betty in the red dog truck to eat the sandwiches I had made or make some for themselves and then eat them. Then it was time for a few hours sleep before morning when we get up and do it all over again.

The morning routine always, and the evening one often, were followed by David and Betty picking up the long (ice cold) dog chains and packing them into the buckets for David to carry over and heft up into the back of the big equipment truck.

✖ It usually took a good three hours to do the job that we call "dropping the dogs". This was always done in the evening after dark and in the morning before the sun arose because we had to use every daylight hour for travel.

Sunday, December 16, 2001........ in the evening

Well... we did not get out of Alberta, Canada. Between the lateness of our start and the slow pace that the big truck required, we only got to Grande Prairie. Here we set up behind a large gas station. There is an all night restaurant next door. The young men who work in the gas station are very pleasant. They allow us to get water for the dogs. Later they come outside and meet some of the dogs out on the chains. They even bring dog biscuits with them. We take a few pictures.

One thing that is very interesting, is the mural painted

on the side of the restaurant. It is a picture of a dog team. I cannot resist taking a photograph of it.

Monday, December 17, 2001............. morning.

During the night I woke up several times to see what appeared to be a raging blizzard outside. Douglas and I are sleeping in the big truck facing Betty and David in the dog truck. We left the picket lines stretched out between the trucks in hopes of saving some time in the morning. When it becomes light enough to consider getting up, the storms have passed. The actual snow on the ground is only about 1 inch more than it was last night. Apparently most of the storms were wind not snowfall. However, that much is enough to cause us a problem. Someone drove in while we were sleeping and parked a car between the two trucks. He parked right on top of all our picket lines. If we try to put the dogs on them, his pretty little car is toast. Between the dogs and the chains, the paint on the little red car would be pretty well shredded. We retire to the restaurant for a conference.

The first order of business is for Betty to call the bank, back in Michigan, to put a hold on any possible rental truck payment. They were not supposed to make a withdrawal until we turned the truck in when we get to our destination. Upon telephoning, Betty discovers that they have already drawn out thousands of dollars. According to the bank records they must have done that not long after I drove the truck out of their lot. We are all upset about that. Then the bank informs Betty that they have already tried to get more money this morning but that section of the bank was not open yet. Betty wants to keep them from taking any more money without permission. The only way the bank can legally refuse them is if she closes the account entirely. She does that. This is an inconvenience because we were going to use this account for some travel expenses. Oh well... we will make do.

DON'T <u>EVER</u> GIVE UP

Betty mentions the cartoon with the frog and the large bird that advises, "Never give up!"

Does that make the truck more illegal than it was before? Am I now driving a stolen truck?

When we get back outside, we find that that the red car has not moved. We cannot find the owner. Rather than damage that person's property, we disengage the chains and carefully pull them out from under that car. We fill all our water jugs at the gas station and drive across the street. There, in a large shopping center parking lot, we drop the dogs. When Tundra returns to his throne in the back seat of the truck I give him the takeout container of leftover Chinese food. Keeping it next to the door was just like having it in a refrigerator. It still smells delicious. He appears to enjoy it as much as he has all the leftovers I have been bringing out for him every time we eat at a restaurant.

It is rather late in the morning as we watch the dogs playing while the sun comes up. They are still beautiful ! !

We continue on our journey. It is not far from Grande Prairie to Dawson Creek and our next province line. We stop at the edge of Dawson Creek for some supplies. We also stop at the General Motors/Chevrolet dealership. David wants to get parts to fix some problems that have occurred with the dog truck. The lights are still not perfect, but just as important, the heater is not working right. It will not run at low speeds. Either it is going hot and full force or it is off. It is an inconvenience but not an insurmountable one. Good thing too, because the parts needed to fix that are not available. We don't care to wait a week or so for them to come in.

Without the bank cards to use, David decides to go to a bank here and change some currency into Canadian money. I have him change some for me too. Then we drive over and down a hill and through the pleasant town of Dawson Creek. At the edge of town there is a large traffic circle. As we are on it preparing to turn on to the next highway (route 97) I see a large sign announcing that this is also the beginning of the Alaska highway. Hooray!!

This is the highway that will lead us directly to Alaska! According to my map before we drove through the town we crossed the province line and are now in British Columbia.

We are leaving Dawson creek. We arrive at a truck inspection station for entering the province of British Columbia. The uniformed officials here are pleasant, helpful and informative. We will need a permit for driving this truck through British Columbia. To get a permit we need the truck registration. Uh Oh....

Partly for appearances and partially because we still hope we were mistaken, we search the truck one more time. We have no more luck finding the registration paper than we expected to. We show the rental contract to the tall red-headed official. We ask if they can use the vehicle identification number for the permit. He says that is not acceptable but since we have a contract he can simply call the rental company and get the registration numbers from them. The company can fax them a copy of the registration form.   Uh Oh...again. I find myself wondering what the jails in British Columbia are like. There is no point in denying that we know the telephone number because it is written in huge numbers across the side of the truck.

I try to make small talk as the official dials the number. I tell him about the many times we have tried to call this number for assistance. We have never made any real contact. We were always switched from one computer-generated recording to another and another and another. Then we would get a voicemail that asked us to hold for a person to assist us. While on hold we would be subjected to some horrible music... if you could call it that. First we'd hear some extremely stylized and badly sung Christmas carols, which were followed by some more traditional Christmas carols that were sung by people who positively could not sing. I like Christmas carols...especially in late December... but not these. The term "could not carry a tune in a bucket" comes to mind. These are interrupted suddenly by a dial tone. At first the relief of hearing something, anything actually on key is a big improvement. It was usually several seconds of appreciating this before we realize we had been hung up on. That is what happened every time one of us tried to call the 800 number.

The uniformed officer listens to me speak with a rather quizzical look on his face and one ear to the receiver of the telephone. His expression suddenly changes. One eyebrow goes down. He winces. He looks as if he's in pain. He says, "I say what you mean"

I say "... the singing?"

He nods. He stands there with the painful look gradually deepening. Then he bursts into laughter and hangs up the telephone. I ask if he got the dial tone. He says, ""No, I got a recording that said, "We are not available to the phone right now. You can leave a message if you like, but we probably won't call you back.""

With that every stern-looking official in the place briefly roars with laughter. Then the red-head with the now-laughing eyes manages to look over the truck and come up with enough information to issue a permit.

I think I will like British Columbia.

Before we drive away from Dawson Creek, someone informs David that we had better get some tire chains for the great big bare tires on the rental truck. We will be needing them to drive 15 tons of truck through the Canadian Rockies on top of that ice and snow. As usual, we lose a huge amount of time and even more money than we can afford locating and purchasing chains for tires almost as tall as I am.

Then we continue on our way. We get as far as Fort St. John, British Columbia, then the light has faded and it is time to drop the dogs.

I have been noticing something that at first had me rather troubled. I enjoy people and hearing them talk. Because of my varied background, I am used to hearing a great variety of accents and dialects. To me, a big part of the fun of traveling is listening to the sounds of each place I visit. Those in nature and those with people.

Many US comedians have made jokes about a Canadian speech characteristic. It is the habit of saying something and then saying "eh?" after it. I don't consider it funny. As a matter of fact I think it is charming. It is sort of like saying "right?" after a statement to be sure you understand what the person was trying to communicate to you. If anything I think of it as being automatically considerate.

I also think of both Betty and David as being polite and considerate people themselves. That is why I was troubled and somewhat confused when I heard David talking with a Canadian who exhibited this characteristic. As he was talking and David was replying, it sounded as if David were mimicking his speech pattern.

"You go over here, eh? and then it takes you to this, eh? and then you wind up over there ,eh...."

"Oh I see what you mean, hey... We need to do this, hey....before we can do that and get to go there, hey..."

I listened with growing discomfort.... and then confusion... People don't take kindly to insults, you know... As I listened, however, I did not notice the person getting irritated.

Very confusing.

I have seen this pattern several times as we have traveled across this vast and beautiful country. A few times I even thought I heard Betty participating in it. Even more confusing. I could not imagine either of these nice people needling someone just to do it. One of the most confusing parts of this whole thing was the fact that I seemed to be the only person even aware it was going on.

Midst all the tension and stress at the province entry station it seemed to be going on very much. When we went into the automotive supply place for the tire chains it was even more so. Suddenly I had a breakthrough ... I was misinterpreting everything. I wasn't listening to "ugly Americans" mocking their fellow Americans to the North. I was listening to a basic Canadian speech pattern being answered by a basic Michigan's Upper Peninsula speech pattern. Betty and David are "Yoopers". (from the U.P.) The "...hey" pattern there is as common (and often as teased about) as the "...eh" pattern is in Canada. I am no longer confused, but now I feel a little foolish.

(I had planned to tell Betty and David of my mistake some time for the laugh, but I never got around to it. I guess they will learn how foolish I was ..at least about that....when they proofread this chapter for the book.)

Tuesday, December 18, 2001

After dropping the dogs this morning, we are on the road again. Betty is very concerned because Tundra did not eat last night. He didn't eat much the night before. Then she discovers that he has been into David and Betty's own food supply. He ate a bag of the carrots they were carrying for snacking. He also munched down a pound or so of their pistachio nuts and a rather large bag of their grapes while they were outside dropping the second and third batches of dogs. As Betty is looking him over thoroughly she discovers that he is lying on her head band. The one she was searching for all over. While she is telling me this and, tongue-in-cheek, accusing me of causing his mischief by spoiling him with leftovers all the time I swear he is behind her with twinkling eyes and barely failing to suppress a grin. She admits she doesn't really care. She loves him anyway and is relieved to know that he is eating.

The travel through the mountains is very slow. I am doing an awful lot of downshifting. Going uphill, this truck does not have the power to pull itself up the steep grade without using lower gears for more torque. Going down the other side I have to keep the speed very low in order to keep the truck under control. For days I have been noticing that the smooth tires seem just as willing to go sideways as they are to go forward. I need to be very careful not to try to brake or to turn too suddenly. Going downhill the weight of this truck is like a giant hand pushing it. I need to control the weight and the speed or we could easily slip off the road and over the side. A person cannot use the brakes to slow or control a truck this size because they would burn out in no time at all. Using the transmission and lower gears for friction is the only way to safely come down a grade. If the roads were straight this would not be as much of a problem as it is but they wind and turn it seems like every foot of the way. As a result, our average speed is probably close to 35 miles per hour.

In the States in mountainous areas there are often road signs that are a picture of a truck heading down a steep incline (decline..?). They are often marked with information stating 3% grade, etc. Outside of Monteagle, Tennessee there is one with a 6% grade. On the way down that one, heading to Chattanooga, there are at least 3 runoff places. These are places where, if someone (usually a trucker) loses the ability to slow or stop his (or her) vehicle the normal way using brakes and/or the transmission, they can drive off the road onto a runaway truck ramp. The ramp is a steep hill going back upwards, constructed of a soft material that would allow a runaway truck to sink into it and stop the truck long before it got anywhere near the far end of the ramp.

While driving the Rockies in Canada, I never saw a hill

marked with a sign less than a 6% grade. The length of the downgrade is also a factor in its hazardousness. I think the one outside Monteagle might be 3 miles. That is really a pretty fair distance. I never saw a runoff ramp the whole time we were in Canada. Actually, Doug's observations of no guard rails that he had made just inside the border held true for our entire drive through that country. I'm not complaining, I want you to know. I just figure that they must expect you to know what you are doing if you choose to drive there. Makes sense to me.

(Just two more comments before I leave this train of thought.

One is that I don't recall if the informational signs that I am mentioning were all the way to the northern border. I do recall that there were a lot of signs that I don't know what information they were supposed to impart because they were completely covered over with snow. I wasn't going to stop and scrape them off to see what they said.

The other comment is that the sign that informed us that we were heading down a 9% grade for 7 miles did give us pause... It seemed to be pretty accurate, however...)

The dog truck and trailer have better tires and are better equipped for this job. In fact it is better for that truck to go faster than my truck can. David usually drives on a little bit ahead and stops to wait for us at a wide or level area. With the ups and down and twists and turns David and Betty and the dogs are frequently out of sight.

As we are driving the remoteness and beauty of this country are breathtaking. Everywhere the hills surrounding us are covered with many feet of pristine snow. The dark green of the pine trees reach straight and strong as though they intend to touch the clear blue sky. I need to pay attention to driving. I watch the road carefully and feel the truck around every turn, shifting gears often, I am careful to miss absolutely no driving information. Yet the beauty all around me is enfolding my consciousness.

I automatically watch for wildlife. Unfortunately, the first moose I see is lying by the roadside, a traffic victim. So is the second, and the third. Then I see a small herd of caribou. It is really a thrill for me. I have never seen them in the wild before. Occasionally I see ravens fly. I finally get a chance to see a large bull moose walking through the snow not far from the road. No wonder they have such incredibly long legs!

As we are traveling we see the dog truck up ahead. David and Betty are both standing on the road. As we near them I see yet another moose traffic victim lying alongside the roadway. This one must be fresh and hasn't had time to freeze. There are several ravens taking advantage of a free meal. I roll slowly up to David as he walks back to me.

"Did you see it ?" He asks me as I roll down the window.

"See what ?"

" The wolf, the black wolf. Betty noticed it first. There it is. Back there... in the trees."

I could only see it as a shadow among the trees. We waited to see if it would come back. Betty walked back up the road toward it. I saw her raise her camera. I heard her voice float through the crisp cold air but I could not hear her words.

That night she wrote about the incident.

"I was crying about Wolf today, asking God to send me another sign. I was writing about him, bawling, looked up and saw a knight wolf.... got out... He stood there looking at me. I took three pictures... thanked the lord and told wolf ... God bless you.. I love you. He then went into the trees happy and free."

We continue driving. Our progress is slow. When it is twilight a huge lynx runs across the highway a little bit in front of the dog truck. It stops just off of the road. As I drive past, it is so close that I can see the tufts of hair at the tops of its ears. It is gorgeous. I have never seen one so large before.

It is dark as we drive into Fort Nelson and look for a place to drop the dogs and spend the night. The town itself seems to be built into the mountainside. It is all ups and downs with really no level place. It is dark as we seek a place with a large enough area and sufficient lighting. We finally decide to spend the night in a motel that will allow us to use their parking lot. While David and Betty are dropping the dogs, I find a late night restaurant that delivers. I think I have ordered half of the menu. It has been a long tiring day. We seem to drop to sleep almost immediately. At least I do. (Later Tundra cashes in on the fact that we are really too tired to even eat.)

Wednesday, December 19, 2001
Morning;

Betty writes: "It was very cold last night... ten degrees below zero. The dogs are steaming in their boxes, shedding their coats. It makes me worry because I want them to have good coats for the outside conditions in Alaska. The babies are bored. They want to go. They have been so good and adjusted better than I ever thought. Galena was playing with her bowl and had it flipped up on her head like a cap. Elim and Kotzebue were playing. She was crawling all over him as he was the digging in the snow.

"Oh No! David says his lens fell out of his glasses. This is the second time that happened. This is the last pair of glasses David has. We will never buy glasses from that place again. We have had problems since we got them and the company will not replace them. We superglued the lenses in but I guess in this cold nothing will hold. We will have to call the doctor back home and order new ones.

"Now we are worried. Can I drive through the mountains with a trailer? The weather is good, thank the Lord, but I still prayed to Jesus to "Please let me find the lens before we go." I said a prayer in my own words and I prayed the Our Father.

"David said, "Let's go. You will never find it. Get in the truck we're ready to leave.""

I said softly, "Please, Jesus"

I saw heat coming from the ground, walked over, stuck my frozen hands in the snow, and picked up the lens the size of a 50 cent piece. Thank you Jesus. I should know by now God will always take care of me.

Today is Isis' birthday. We will sing happy birthday and get her a cheeseburger cake."

Evening

It was slow going today. We drove a grand total of 122 miles. The drive was slow. Those tires are frustrating. Every time I tried to get some speed rolling on the straight-aways the back end would like to pass the front. Our top speed, on the rare occasions when we reached it, was 35 mph. We did see a caribou herd... and then a little further on right by the road there were two more of them.

Several times during the day we were driving near some of the summits and the side windows on the truck would ice up. With the defrosters on and going full-blast the windshield stayed clear but only the front couple of inches of the side windows became less obscured. The rest of them were covered

with ice.... not fog... not frost.... ice.

We have stopped for the night at the Toad River Lodge here in British Columbia. The people are very pleasant. While David and Betty are dropping the dogs, one of the people here gives me some recipes for crunchy snacks.

We have seen many signs about bears in the past few days. I'm sure they are for effect on tourists. However, there would be no humor to them if they didn't also ring true. I'll try to give you the essence of them here;

~Travelers should be aware that this is considered bear country. There are two basic kinds of bears in this part of the country. Black bears and brown bears (*brown bears are what people in the States call Grizzly bears*). It is a good idea to be able to tell them apart. Black bears are smaller and more nimble. If you climb a tree to get away from a black bear he can run right up it after you. Brown bears are bigger and they cannot climb trees. If you climb a tree to get away from a brown bear, he will push it over to get you.

To be safe from bears many travellers wear bells to warn bears of their approach so as not to startle them. They also carry pepper spray to fend them off.

It is also a good idea to be able to tell which bear country you might be in by being able to identify bears by their scat. (That which bears do in the woods.) Black bear scat is large and crumbly and contains bits of feathers, berry seeds, and twigs. Brown bear scat is larger and often contains bells and smells like pepper.~

David and Betty come in, buy a cheeseburger and go outside again. They are feeding it to Isis and singing happy birthday. It figures. Today Isis is fourteen years old. She enjoys her party.

When David and Betty come inside, they talk about how cold it is. The radio reports that it is 40 degrees below zero. David's feet became very cold. He will have to change his sweat socks before he goes to sleep.

Thursday, December 20, 2001

It was so cold outside last night that we had to keep the rental truck running all night. One good thing that I can say for it, is that that heater works well. When I awakened David and Betty already had dogs out on the lines. They have the dogs taken care of and ready to go way before it is light.

It is very hard to drive that truck when I cannot see the twists and turns of the road ahead. I offer to buy breakfast.

Betty says to ask David. Later she writes in her journal that she should have known better. David loves food so much that he says yes.

When we do start driving, it is still twilight. Before we started out, Betty told me that she had given the truck a name. She calls it the Glitch.... because most of the time when there is a glitch in our plans, that's what is in the center of it. I certainly can't argue with that!

One thing that I have been noticing when people in this part of the country are talking, is that they never use the word mountain. They say hills. It is three hills to the next roadside stop. There are two good hills before the next town. We continue waddling the glitch up and down these hills.

As we are driving in this incredible beauty we spot a herd of buffalo. A little further on we spy a lone bull on the top of a hill. I wouldn't have expected to see these creatures that I associate with the rolling hills of South Dakota in this part of the world on top of the Canadian Rockies, but here they are.

It took most of the day but we have finally crossed into Yukon Territory around 3:00 PM. We cross the provincial line between Yukon Territory and British Columbia several times for the rest of the afternoon. At a pit stop in Yukon Territory someone mentions that is about two good hills to the bridge. We have crossed a lot of bridges in the past week or so. Somehow the person's tone of voice when they say "the bridge" seems to put quotation marks around it.

We continue.

The road has deteriorated to a dirt track under the packed snow.

In the farm country where I live, sometimes canals run through the farm fields. When the farmers want to cross from one field to another they often form their own bridges across those canals. They do this by dropping two beams or railroad ties across them and then filling in the space between with whatever lumber they have around.

As I am rolling down a heart-in-your-throat steep hill, I look down at something that makes the farmer bridges look like the Golden Gate in San Francisco! ... "The bridge"

I didn't dare look left or right. I aim for the middle of the bridge and hold my breath. I hope that if the outer wheels hang over, at least the inner wheels will stay on the bridge and get us across.

We survive and continue to drive. Today our absolute top speed was 35 mph. We only reached that once. We are all troubled by our lack of progress. I wish I could push this truck faster but I can't do it and stay on the road.

It is amazing. We have been driving through scenes of indescribable beauty for days. It is impossible to become impervious to it. And still... surrounded by all this... we round a curve to reveal yet another scene so gorgeous that it makes us gasp! This keeps on happening!!

At Watson Lake, Yukon Territory, we pass another weight station. The sign says for commercial vehicles to stop. So we don't. David pulls into an auto parts store to try to find the part for his truck heater. When he comes out he declares that we are going on. He wants to make it to Morley River or maybe even Teslin tonight. I object, telling him that in the dark I can't see what the road ahead is like so I don't know when to downshift, and I can't see if there is gravel, or what the road conditions are like, so I can't judge what would be a safe speed or what would be the tires ability to hold the road. David insists on going. This is the first time we have disagreed on anything. I really feel as strongly he does that this trip is taking far too long.

I continue to follow... slowly and carefully. David pulls over and comes back to us. He says he'll drive the rental truck and Betty can drive their truck. He says the Doug should go up and ride with Betty.

I tell him I don't plan to die on a Canadian highway.

He says, "you won't"

I say, "or sailing off of one either!"

He says, "don't worry"

I say, "then take me to the nearest airport, right now!"

He walks back to his truck and talks with Betty. He returns to get the dog chains out of the back of my truck. He says they will continue and have the dogs dropped by the time we get there. I say OK. They go on ahead.

As we continue the light snow suddenly becomes more intense. It is getting harder and harder to see. A semi truck passes us and its backwash temporarily totally blinds us. We get as far as a junction (highway 37) with a gas station and store. There stands David in the road waving us in. It is impossible to say how glad I am to see that!

By the time we have the trucks situated and the chains out, what appeared to have been a full blown blizzard has totally gone away. Strange!

As usual my hands seize up in the cold. So I go inside and do a little souvenir shopping for the gang back home. (There is a jade mine a little way down highway 37). I sit in the truck and make sandwiches and write in this journal.

I watch Betty and David taking care of their dogs. Each one is treated not only as an individual but as someone special. I think it is even colder than last night but David and Betty do not take even one shortcut. Everybody gets complete and total care.

Doug gets out and walks Dehlia and then Tundra. We are all glad to see that because he is having trouble with his feet swelling up due to inactivity. Sometimes he takes off his boots and can't get them back on again. It is good to see that his boots are on. Walking the dogs not only helps David and Betty, it is very good for Doug. When he is finished with that, I notice almost with some amusement, as this 81 year old man that needed two people to push him up into the truck in Michigan virtually vaults right from the ground to get back into the nice warm cab next to me.

Betty comes over and tells me that she is worried about Isis. She is stiff and doesn't want to move. She seems to have trouble breathing. Her breath is cold...

Once again we feel helpless. The most I can do is to blow as much hot air as I can from the truck heater into the sleeping bag I have been using. I offer it to Betty to wrap-around Isis. She accepts it. It is worth a try. I think we both know that it is futile, but we won't pass even a remote chance.

We have been on the road way too long!

Friday, December 21, 2001

It is morning again. It is still dark. David comes to me and asks me to check Isis. He says that he believes she is gone but wants me to double check. Because I am an EMT he feels that I can check her medically. I walk with him to the dog box. She looks peaceful. One look at her eyes tells me that no one is there. David and Betty just want scientific confirmation of what they already know in their hearts. I do a couple of perfunctory tests. Then we are all satisfied but no one is happy about it. Betty tells me that she waited until this morning to say goodbye to mom and dad.

I am racked with guilt. Logically I know and understand that I cannot possibly push that truck any harder or any faster than I have been. But I feel the way I feel and it is something I will always carry with me.

I'm angry with the truck. We could do nothing about Wolf. I think that we all feel that it was just his time. But Isis... no, this should not have happened.

Betty writes in her journal :
"The first day of winter. Isis is dying. We stay with her and say our goodbyes. She is gone. My heart thinks this trip has broken us in more ways than one. Only the dogs' spirits and with God's help, can we go on. I know God is with us. We pray many times a day."

Betty tells me that Isis has gone to be with her beloved Bandit whom she missed so dearly.

After dog care, we get back on the road and head for Whitehorse, Yukon Territory.

Traveling in this province seems to be going a little better. The roads have improved a little and there seems to be a little more gravel on them. This is a big help! I am getting excited as we attain 45 mph for the first time in days. Then we hit 50... once even 55 mph! We are making much better time. There are only a few places that while we are driving the side windows ice up... even with the defrosters going full blast. In the past few days, this has happened several times at high altitudes.

When we cross the continental divide Betty and David are ahead of us and out of sight. Too bad. I wanted to take a picture of them with the continental divide signs. Douglas leans out of his window and snaps a photograph anyway. Then we continue on.

In the afternoon we have a pit stop at Morley river. We order and eat some delicious pie in honor of Doug's birthday tomorrow. Then we hit the road again.

We arrive in Whitehorse well after dark. According to the brochures we pick up, this city is named after the rapids on the Yukon river whose white spumes seem to look like the manes and tails of running horses. We locate a place across the highway from the airport and drop the dogs. Either Betty or David telephones the only malamute breeder that they know to be in the area. He comes out to visit during the dog drop. He seems to like the looks of the dogs and is very encouraging to Betty and David. Hans Oettli has run Malamutes for many years so he is very knowlegable and his opinion is appreciated.

Saturday, December 22, 2001

We are up and out of Whitehorse fairly early. The dog dropping is going quite smoothly. Betty and David work like a well oiled machine. If Doug or I can help them it is nice but they have everything pretty much down to a science and flow through the business of care without missing a beat. Even with such precision it still takes about the same amount of time because each dog still receives its full measure of attention. We get on the road hoping to spend tonight in Alaska.

Today is Doug's 81st birthday. He spent one birthday in his youth at one army training camp. Another one at a base across the country, and one on a South Pacific island. We are all trying for him to be able to spend this one in Alaska.

We do our best but the hills and the road conditions have not improved enough for us to quite make it to the border. We see elk off to one side of the road. These big guys are not the size of moose... but they are a pretty close second. They are magnificent strolling through snow that must be about 4 feet deep.

We spend much of the day zig zagging up and down the mountain range that goes right to the banks of a huge lake. There appears to be only the width of the road we are on between them. To one side of us rocky cliffs rise straight up. To the other is either the lake or a long straight drop directly to the lake. It is interesting, awesome, and beautiful. What it is not is fast traveling. We do our best but decide to stop when we get to Beaver Creek, Y.T.

The lodge there is very picturesque. It is a huge log structure with both wilderness-type and Christmas-type decorations outside. Inside it is a store, a souvenir shop, a bakery, and of course a restaurant and kitchen. All of this decorated liberally with actual stuffed wild game. There is a full-grown stuffed musk ox just inside the front door. Over the door that leads to the kitchen is a sign declaring the age and originator of their sourdough starter, something I know to be a point of pride in this part of the world. The older your sourdough, the better. This one dates from the 1800's.

The people there are not too keen on us dropping dogs in their front parking lot so they give us a multiple-room accommodation way to the rear area. Fine with us.

Before we drop dogs and settle into our rooms we decide to have dinner. (Before we even get seated in the huge log walled dining room, I have a quick word with the woman who runs the bakery and the souvenir shop and the motel sign-in and who will be our waitress tonight. People here are versatile, I guess... no, I'm sure).

In the dining room I mention to Betty about the sign over the kitchen door. She says that she has never had any sourdough bakery. One of the menu items is a muskox burger. We order ours on the sourdough bread. I order mine rare and it is delicious. Betty prefers hers done and enjoys it too. The men opt for the beef stew which is mostly beef. Maybe meat is easier to acquire and store around here than fresh vegetables. Whatever the reason, a person sure gets good value on a meal here. The waitress brings more sourdough bread to accompany the stew. I think even David eats his fill.

102

Then at a nod from me the waitress appears with a huge piece of carrot cake with a birthday candle burning in it. We all sing Happy Birthday to Doug. The waitress comments that he may not be in Alaska yet, but celebrating his birthday on the Klondike in the Yukon is OK too. I think Doug agrees.

The owner of the place comes over and talks with David. He seems interested in the goal of the Iditarod with the Malamutes. He says that no one up here runs the "big dogs" any more. David obviously enjoys telling him that he feels his team has what it takes to do it.

Later we head back to our rooms. Betty is concerned because Doug's feet are swollen from sitting too long inactive in that darn Glitch. She gives him some herbal gel to rub on them after his bath. He does it and drops off almost instantly to sleep. In the morning he will put on the fluffy new socks that Betty and David gave him for his birthday.

The room arrangement is such that I get one of the beds in the big bedroom. Betty and David will share the other. I briefly hope that it will not be awkward. I needn't have worried. I am zonked out asleep long before they come in. They could swing from the rafters and do handsprings all over the room while yodeling for all I know.

One of the reasons that they are so late coming in is because Artic has gotten sick in his dogbox. Betty gives him herbs and feeds him just venison to settle his stomach. Then she spends the next three hours getting him and his box cleaned up. In this cold everything freezes so it is hard to scrape off. But if it wasn't cleaned up thoroughly when Artic returned to his box, his body heat would thaw it and make it and him pretty nasty. Ugh! As it is she spends a lot of that time getting him and his coat cleaned up. He acts as though he is much happier when she is finished. She makes sure that he gets an extra big drink of fresh water before he goes in for the night. In the morning he is one of the first to come out. He has been ok in there and not had any more accidents overnight. His body functions are much nearer normal already. He gets more herbs and fresh water this morning. He appears to be a little perkier.

A lot of people that have talked to Betty and David have told them that dogs coming "up here" get sick on the way up and get sick just being in the new environment. It usually takes from a few weeks to a few months for their immune systems to build up. Even dogs that live here all the time often get sick every winter with viruses .

Betty has decided to try to keep track of how well her dogs do (or don't do) because she has tried to maintain a good regimen of vitamin, mineral and herbal supplementation. With the dogs of her own breeding, the herbal building was started before they were born. She will try to document the effects of the diet, herbs and breeding program because hers are different from anyone else's.

Of course, she never discounts her faith in God's help in this whole endeavor.

(It is only after I have returned to the lower 48 and am reading her journal that I discover that she spent much of the day sleeping as David drove because she was not feeling well. A lot of it has to do with being bruised and stiff from when the Glitch tried to throw her into traffic that one night way back in Alberta. I think that most of the time this lady operates on will-power and pure courage.)

Sunday December 23, 2001

In the morning we slept until after 7:30. Everyone seems refreshed by showers and actually sleeping in beds. While David and Betty drop the dogs, I walk to the lodge and come back with two sacks full of bakery. We munch some of it as we are preparing to leave. The rest is for snacking while we are on the road. Actually, David is the one that snacks a lot while he drives. I do believe that man has nibbled his way across Canada.

(Actually, it turns out that Tundra is a pretty good match for David. By this stage of the trip, he had consumed snacks of Chinese food, trimmings and leftovers (no bones), from pork chops, a big container of french fries covered with gravy and meat, apparently an area specialty in B.C. , and some fruit flavored yogurt, all of which were more or less given to him. He also managed to scrounge up on his own a few more things such as a pound or so of pistachio nuts, almost a pound of baby carrots, a package of apple turnovers, maybe half a dozen, a few blueberry muffins, a tangerine, sans peeling, and four baloney sandwiches, two of which he just ate the meat off of and left the bread for "mom and dad".)

I found a long time ago, I was too busy while I was driving to even consider eating. I really didn't have a hand free to do it. I used both feet for balance and operation of the pedals. I needed both hands on the wheel to navigate around the curves and feel for traction on the road. I needed to use one hand almost constantly to shift and downshift. And while I was at it, on some of those curves and hills, I wanted one hand across my eyes.

After one stop for groceries somewhere back there in Canada, Betty handed me a bag of pistachio nuts. It must have contained about 2 lbs. of them. I gave it back to Betty for them to eat up in the dog truck, while we were somewhere in the Yukon territory. (This was after Tundra had raided their supply.) I had not had time to eat more than about 15 or 20 of them in the days they had been in our truck.

Last night I telephoned home. This morning David and Betty each telephone their families, in Michigan and Wisconsin respectively. Then they telephone the Vaughans to tell them we are coming and getting close.

Before we leave, David changes fuses in the truck again. They are still blowing them and having trouble with the lights. The man here at Beaver Creek says that it is a common problem. Because of changes in the weather, condensation makes the circuits act up and blow fuses. With all the ups and downs we have been doing, and the changes in weather, and air moisture, that certainly does seem to make sense.

We are finally ready and take to the road. We will make it to Alaska today! We will be trying for Anchorage.

Entering Alaska

Sunday December 23, 2001
Evening

OK, so we didn't make it to Anchorage. At least we are finally in Alaska. I am thrilled!

When people hear that I raise Alaskan malamutes, they always ask if I've been to Alaska. Now I can say yes. It is beautiful here. Not that the scenery has been any less than breathtaking for days and days through Canada.

We came through the border patrol station and crossed back into the United States of America with very little trouble.

As usual Betty had all the paperwork in order. The border patrol guard was ready for us as we rolled up behind the dog truck. Again, all that he asked us for was my driver's license and Doug's birth certificate. He didn't really scrutinize any of it. He seemed quite friendly as he agreed with me that Doug and I probably did not look like international terrorists. Then we were back on the road and rolling again.

We still have plenty of mountains and snow to keep our speed down. At Tok David tells me he wants to drive the rental truck and follow Betty driving in the dog truck... which is still having trouble with its lights and blowing fuses. I get to go up and ride with Betty in the front truck. Daylight was very short

term today. When we got on the road around 11:00 AM, it was still twilight. It gradually brightened up for about four hours. Then we had more twilight. It got dark early. Driving in the snow and in the dark is difficult. Betty is a very good driver. However, she has difficulty driving in poor visibility. Thanks to cataracts due to her diabetes. She is very sensible and will not drive faster or further than she can see.

At Tok Junction we make the turn from the Alaska highway (US 2 in Alaska) onto Highway 1 which turns toward Anchorage. As the darkness deepens and driving becomes more difficult we are looking for a place to stop. We try Gulkana but there is no place to drop the dogs, so we continue on to Glennallen. We find sufficient room and conditions at an all night gas station on a corner where Highway 4 heads south to Valdez. We all have gas station microwaved junk food for supper. Yum!

While the dogs are out on their chains, several of the locals come over to get a look at them. One pickup truck with a very big Alaskan malamute drives in, the driver looks at the dogs and then drives out again. Possibly because his malamute wanted to jump out and eat the whole team. He was chained in the truck bed but we were glad to see that the driver did not stick around long enough to see which was stronger, the dog or the chain. David and Betty exchange names and addresses with a guy who says his name is Sourdough Joe.

Most of the people that come out to look at the team don't call them "Malamutes". They just refer to them as "the Big Dogs"

Later Betty tells me she had an interesting talk with a local (Native? Indian?...?) Who said that he used to drive malamutes when he was younger. He said that he likes them. They will go a steady pace "forever."

Before we settle in for the night, David and Betty walk over to me. Each of them tell me that they had been talking to different people. More than one of them mentioned to the Britzs that they were surprised to see the condition that the dogs were in. One or two of them said that usually by the time someone got to this point in their travel, their dogs were exhausted and weak. It was unusual to see them with even the strength to stand up, let alone see these big powerful dogs playing with each other on the picket line and running around playing with David and Betty on leashes. Betty just smiled. She said, "I guess we must be doing something right."

Monday December 24, 2001
Merry Christmas Eve day!!!

As usual, dogs before dawn. We're trying to get a start as early as possible. People tell us that it is 8 hours to Anchorage. (Not at the speed we travel.) We have only about four or five hours of daylight. Oh well, we will keep plugging away at it.

Before we leave, David comes to me and says he needs some parts for the dog chains. Equipment will be different up in the dog yard than it was here on the way up on the picket line. He tells me that most hardware stores do not carry enough items in stock for the job he needs to do, so he will have to stop at several hardware stores along the way. Therefore when I'm driving behind them and they pull off and stop at a hardware store I should keep on driving. Because they have the faster vehicle, they will catch up with me.

We drove out of the lot at 10:20 am. Sure enough, a little way down the road David pulled into a hardware store... I kept going. They must have stopped at more than one store because they did not catch up to us until Eureka.

We had been driving under a gray sky for a few hours. We came to an area that was wide and flat. It was impossible to even guess at the elevation. I think it was like a high flat plateau. I do not know of any way to find out if I am correct.

As we approached Eureka we noticed some very strange things along the road. There were large poles like giant upside down letter L's at regular intervals along both sides of the road. Doug and I speculated on what these might be. At first we believed that they were too far from the edge of the road to be markers for snow plows. With our backgrounds that was the first thing each of us thought of. After we had ruled that out, we bandied about ideas as we approached, passed through, and left behind the settlement Eureka. It finally dawned on us, that we should not be looking at the base of the poles. We should have been looking at the tops. They all ended just at the edge of the road. We were right the first time. When snow on the wide flat area concealed the location of the road, these arms pointed it out. I think that we are both feeling rather smug about solving our little puzzle when the dog truck finally overtakes us. They wave at us as they go by, and we all continue driving.

The flat land begins to be broken up by hills and curves.

110

We are back in what we consider more normal mountainous terrain. The road, the hillsides going up and the hillsides going down, are all white. As we round a white curve around a white hill, the white road in front of us widens out. Somehow at the same time we spot the dog truck stopped ahead of us and probably the most spectacular scene that we have seen in this long parade of day after day breathtaking vistas.

Off to our left drops a huge deep valley. Across that rises a glorious mountain range. It is completely snow-covered and is layers and rows of jagged peaks. At anytime that would have been an outstanding view... even on this trip. But what makes it so glorious is the golden sun breaking through underneath the clouds and actually between the mountains. It is like an explosion of gold between the white rugged peaks. What makes it even more dramatic are the indigo blue shadows every place that the gold does not touch.

David has pulled over and both of them are out of the truck awestruck by the scene. Betty comes back to our truck to get a fresh roll of film. I have long ago used up the last of my little disposable cameras. That's OK. There is no way one of them could capture what we are seeing. I actually doubt if any camera could possibly come even close.

Betty wants to give it a try with her camera. She says even if it cannot capture all of the grandeur, she would like to have a picture to remember our last sunset on the road.

Really hope it does turn out.

Several miles further on we see a sign saying, "Majestic Valley". There can be no mistake about what it is naming.

We continue to drive. The hills become steeper. The curves become sharper. (Remember? When you're viewing them in the distance, they can be called mountains. Actually they are usually called this range or that range, but as we, or you, drive them, the road underfoot or under tire as the case may be, goes up and down hills.)

Whatever you call them, they become steeper and more twisting than they have been before. We seem to be driving through the heart of some of the ruggedest range we have ever seen.

There is a moose standing right next to the road. A little further on two of them run across the road in front of us. Off to our left side now is what appears to be a wide frozen river. Beyond that is a huge glacier. We drive with it at our side for a long time. Though it remains in sight, we continue twisting up and down sharp steep hills. Every now and then we pass what appears to be a little parking area in the middle of nowhere. As we pass one, I see a man standing next to his own dog truck. I cannot tell if he is getting ready to leave or has just returned. It doesn't really matter. It is exciting just to be in this country.

There are times and places as we waddle this cumbersome truck up and down the hills where our speed is reduced to five mph. As busy as I am, I can still feel the rugged beauty all around me. I feel that it is soaking into me from all directions.

After hours of this kind of driving, the hills gradually become gentler. The road widens. Pretty soon it actually seems to be a highway. About this time I realize two important facts. The first, though the less important, is the fact that the glorious gold we saw up the mountains was not a sunset at all. At about 1:00 in the afternoon, we had pulled over to watch our first sunrise in Alaska!

The second, was the fact that we had not seen Betty, David or the dog truck since then.

As usual, our answer is to continue to drive. Soon we are traveling on a highway, one that has been plowed down to the blacktop, one that has lanes, with lines designating what they are. It is a real treat to be able to drive on such a road. We are able to drive normal highway speeds. Now Anchorage doesn't seem so far.

We still have not located the Britz's or the dog truck. We know that they have talked to the Vaughans on the telephone. I think they're supposed to meet them in Wasilla. From the looks of the map, we are not terribly far from

Anchorage.

We enter a town named Palmer. There is a crossroad there that according to the sign is a direct route to Wasilla. It would be nice to take a short cut. Since we don't know where Betty and David are, we decide we should continue on this road all the way to the main junction shown on the map. So we continue through Palmer toward Anchorage. In less than 10 miles we get to the turnoff, Highway 3, which will take us to Wasilla. This is also one of the main highways in this part of the state. In fact, they are some of the main roads in the whole state if my trusty rusty road atlas is to be believed. Now we are heading north and west. Anchorage is somewhere to the south. We stay on the main road driving fairly slowly through Wasilla. I didn't realize the town was this big. I thought it would be easy to locate Betty and David. The dog truck and trailer should stand out. We continue looking, in gas stations, in the parking lots of stores.

Perhaps they have gone on ahead by now. Throughout this whole trip we have all felt that we should be getting further faster than we have been. Now the goal is close. Perhaps they feel the same urge that I have. We have been aiming for that little spot on the big map for so long I just want to get there. After all, David did say to continue and they would catch up to us.

According to the map, Trapper Creek is not much further. It is a much smaller community. Maybe they continued, knowing they could find us more easily in a smaller town. For want of something better to do, we continue to head for our goal.

As we drive along the outskirts of Wasilla the light is beginning to fade. The long Alaska dusk is beginning. In someone's front yard I notice a full grown moose nibbling away at small twigs on a tree. It seems totally unbothered by the neighborhood around it or the traffic going past quite closely. As Douglas and I are remarking about that we pass another one in an identical situation.

When we stop for fuel we ask about Trapper Creek.

We are told to just continue on park highway, we can't miss it. Everyone we talk to calls this the Parks Highway* ...even before we turned onto it. Some of the people from right in the area were unaware that it even had a number name. Driving north we cross the tracks for the Alaska railroad, three times. There is the turnoff for Talkeetna. We have already driven past Willow. All the names of places in the paragraphs I have just written are places and names that I have heard or read about. Before they were just words or printing on a map. Now they are real to me. For good or bad, we are here.

* *(It is only months after I have returned to the lower 48, on a day when it was 100 degrees in the shade, that I look again at my map of that area. I discover much to my chagrin, that the highway which I mention, is actually named the George Parks Highway. I had thought that people were referring to Denali National Park, on that highway between Anchorage and Fairbanks.)*

A little north of Talkeetna we drive into the parking lot of the restaurant and gas station. It is late for us. Usually by the time it is this dark, about half of the dogs are already dropped. I think if we park the truck where it can be seen easily from the road, we should spend the night and let Betty and David find us. I go into the restaurant to ask if it's OK. They're preparing to close, after all it's Christmas Eve. They say we can stay if we want but Trapper Creek is just a few more mile markers north. 13 miles? 15 miles? I thank them. After a short conference in the truck Doug and I decide we may as well go all the way to Trapper Creek. That has been the goal of this whole trip. Why stop now?

As we continue sometimes it seems like those mile markers are pretty far apart. Sometimes we also seem to miss a few. But finally we arrive in Trapper Creek. I am sure we have arrived because the building that we stop in front of has a big sign that says Trapper Creek Inn.

We have one more conference in the truck. I would like

to park the truck near the road where it can be spotted easily, and sleep in it. David and Betty can find us now or in the morning. Doug however would like the comfort of staying at the Inn. That is really not unreasonable. He is still having trouble with swollen feet. Sleeping sitting up in the truck is really not helping. Here we sit right in front of a motel. I am tempted myself. When Doug offers to pay for the room, that tips the scale.

He comes out with the room key and the information that the Inn is now closing and will remain so until after Christmas. Then he says we are supposed to drive the truck around to the back parking lot. From there it is three flights up to our room. I had wanted to leave the truck in front but if we are going to be out of it maybe it is better to allow it to idle out of sight overnight.

I am somewhat surprised to find that the three flights up to our room are an outside wooden staircase. There is coffee and a pot in the room. With this and the leftover munchies from Beaver Creek, we have our Christmas Eve dinner and promptly drop off to sleep.

Tuesday December 25, 2001
Merry Christmas from Trapper Creek Alaska!!!

Not exactly where I had expected to spend Christmas morning, but what the heck. An adventure is an adventure.

I walk downstairs to use the outside telephone. It is in an old fashioned phonebooth, one with no door. It was apropos however because the telephone is pretty much like the rest of this trip. I try to use my telephone card to call home and wish everyone a merry Christmas and to brag just a little about finally being in Alaska. I can't use my card because all of the circuits are busy. The telephone promptly eats all my change. A man comes up on a snow machine and trys to help but he can't get his card to work either. He says he is leaving his machine here and hitch hiking a few miles to the south to pick up party supplies for the holiday. He will be back later. Actually he's heading for the place where we'd asked for direc-

115

tions last night. I wonder if they are open today. While he is hitching and I am standing in the telephone booth, a full grown moose trots out of the woods and onto the highway. A small pickup truck coming from the north passes my friend hitching but has to slow down for the moose. It looks around and then casually trots off.

Meanwhile, I have dug around in my pockets and found some more change. I telephone a number from the phone book whose address is Petersville Road. That is the road that goes to the left from Parks Highway. I can see the beginning of it from where I stand. It is also the road to the Vaughan's cabin. The person on the phone gives me the number of a person who can give me the telephone number to the Vaughan's cabin. That may sound a little roundabout to people from the lower 48, but by golly it works. Soon I am speaking to Carolyn Vaughan.

She tells me that David and Betty are still in Wasilla looking for us. I tell her where we are. She says she expects them to call back. I say to tell them we will stay put until they catch up to us. She suggests that I call back later. I tell her that I can, only if Doug has any quarters.

When I call back later on, she informs me that David and Betty are on their way to us. Then I tell her that I am driving the equipment truck. She informs me that the first 3 miles of Petersville Road are paved. She suggests we stop at the end of that and put the chains on.

So far we have not used the tire chains. They can be used to only at speeds of under 20 mph. Although we have been traveling slowly, we were not traveling quite that slowly. There were one or two hills that were pretty bad, but David would carefully drive ahead to check them. Then he would drive back to us waiting in the big truck, and tell us about the conditions. He was obviously a very good judge of those conditions. He could make suggestions about how to waddle that big truck safely down those hills. He must have been pretty good at it because here we are.

Betty and David meet us there at the Inn. We all then

proceed. Up? Down? Out? Petersville Road. When we get to the end of the pavement and start down the gravel and dirt road I discover that driving conditions are actually better. The gravel that has worked its way up through the snow gives these big bald tires better traction than they have had in quite a while. Of course we traverse several hills. We were warned about a bad one just before the last parking lot. As we approach it we stop both trucks, get out, walk up to it and look it over. David offers to drive the dog truck down and then walk back and drive the big truck down. I have come this far. I tell him, "Just don't stop in front of me!" As he walks back to the dog truck I am not sure if he is shaking his head or chuckling.

We take that hill with no more incident than any other. Then we drive to a great big parking lot. There are quite a few pickup trucks and trailers in considerable variety parked in this lot, and there is still a huge amount of room to park. We pull in, turn around and park facing the road. On the other side of the road there is a gorge and then of course another hill. It is obvious that the road continues past the parking lot, slopes down, crosses a bridge over the gorge and climbs that hill. It is equally obvious that the road from this point on is not plowed. There is no way that this big truck is going any further tonight.

Before long a snow machine approaches. Carolyn Vaughan has come to meet us. She drives up to Betty and David. I climb down out of the truck to meet her also. As she turns toward us I am struck by a pair of startlingly blue eyes, the only part of her not engulfed by winter clothing. What an attention-getter!

Since the dog truck has good tires and four wheel drive, it is decided that Doug will join David and Betty in it and they will all follow Carolyn to the Vaughan's cabin. There they can unload the dogs and take care of them. I volunteer to stay with the big truck overnight. They can come out and get me in the morning. Maybe I can fly out of Anchorage and be home by this time tomorrow. With that thought I am quite content to spend another night in this truck. It will seemed quite roomy without Doug and his sleeping bag.

In Alaska

Friday, December 28, 2001

It has been way too long since I've written anything in this journal. I apologize to it and to myself and will try to fill in that huge gap. On Christmas night I had just settled in with a book on tape, a piece of Beaver Creek bakery, and paper to write a farewell letter to my friend David wishing him well on this tremendous endeavor, and reminding - no strongly urging him to be sure to use his greatest asset, Betty. I believe that somewhere in there I even made reference to Sacajewea.

Just after Betty and David had gone, a young man in a pickup truck drove up to the Glitch and talked to me. He told me that my friends were nearing the cabin and had asked him to stop and pick up some barrels. He was presently on his way into town and would stop for them on the way back. When he did come back with a friend, he also talked me into riding with them to the cabin to meet with Betty and David. He said that Doug was already there. (I found out after I had returned to the lower 48 that Betty had paid him what I consider an obscene amount of money to give me a ride in to the cabins.)

As he drove his high four wheel drive pickup truck down the snow covered pathway, I noticed frequent thumps as if we were hitting something rather solid in the road. When I asked him about this he said they were just moguls, something like waves in the snow formed by snow machines. He said they were getting pretty bad now. Later tonight he would be driving down to Anchorage. Tonight's trip in and out might be the last time he drives this pickup truck down this road this season.

When we had gone several miles we came upon David and Betty and Carolyn. They were dropping the dogs in what looked like a little clearing among some trees. They said they could go no further because the truck-trailer combination was disabled. The young man would take me to the cabin and they would meet me there when they were finished.

After several more miles of driving the young fellow stopped the truck. He said that we were at the top of Col. Norman Vaughan's driveway. He told me all I had to do was to follow it and it would take me to the cabins. I asked about dangerous wild animals, moose for instance. (We had seen so many on the way up and this area seemed a lot more remote.) He said something like, "I suppose some can get pretty mean, but most of them are OK." Somehow, I felt that there was a chuckle in their somewhere.

As I walked the long downhill winding driveway toward the unseen cabins, I wondered if a wild animal was near, and if it was would it consider me an intruder or just a passer by. Then I heard an odd sound to my left up the hill. A rattling? A rustling? No, a rather more vigorous sound. Rattling? No. Rustling? No. Scraping? Shaking? No. Maybe a combination of all of that. Hmmmmm. Closer to correct, but, still... Suddenly the sound stopped. After several seconds it started again. I was so engrossed in trying to imagine not only what was making that sound but how it was making it, that I wasn't afraid of a wild animal, just extremely curious.

I made it to the cabin without incident and was welcomed into its bright cheery atmosphere.

Col. Vaughan is a pleasant and gracious man. He talked of driving the way we had come, many times, from Massachusetts! The first time he did it as a dog handler for Dr. Roland Lombard. Col. Vaughan referred to him as a famous dog musher and a very good person. He obviously has great respect, even admiration for the man. Considering the source, even if I didn't know about him I would be impressed.

We had some time to visit while we were waiting for the others. Somewhere in that time I mentioned the strange sound I had heard while coming down the drive. As I tried to describe it, Col. Vaughan identified my mystical wild animal as the spinning windmill part of the wind generator for his self-contained electrical system.

It was during this visiting time that Col. Vaughan said he

had only one question to ask me about the dogs that Betty and David have. He wanted to know what their feet are like. When I described the strong round feet with well arched toes that could spread out to work as snow shoes but were usually tight and springy, he sort of smiled and sat back appearing to be satisfied with that explanation.

When the others arrived, David and Betty went to put some things in the handlers' cabin. While they were gone, Carolyn whipped up a meal fit for a king in what seemed like mere minutes. We all had a lovely Christmas dinner and enjoyed good company. Much nicer than sleeping alone in a rental truck!

The following day was a busy one. It was spent doing necessary things. Carolyn helped the Britz's to bring in loads of stuff from the trucks. She has a unique snow machine trailer, not one on which to carry a snow machine, one to be towed by a snow machine. It is a toboggan-style invention made from the stuff that we usually use to cover the bottoms of our dogsled runners. It is surprising how much can be carried on it. Even so, the loads that came in were barely scratching the surface of what there is to haul. It is nice to have some of our supplies and clothing, however.

The most important job of the day was to get all of the dogs from the disabled truck and trailer to the cabin. Carolyn had stakes set in for the dogs in the dog yard before we arrived. There were 6 foot high metal stakes that were driven into the ground. These were covered with equally long metal pipes. The height was to keep dog chains from slipping over the tops and freeing the dogs from the tie-outs. Around these pipes one end of a 6 foot long chain was fastened. The dog yard was empty. The dog truck was full. That needed to change.

The night before, while driving in through the deep snow those strange formations called moguls had created so much trouble and uneven jerking on the trailer hitch of the truck that most of the bolts in it had actually torn free. It was now hanging by just a few remaining bolts. For the time being that truck was not hauling any trailer any where.

How to get the dogs in that last several miles was the question. The answer? By dogsled of course! Sixteen days of traveling in dog boxes had taken a serious toll on them. Their previous physical conditioning was severely decreased. And their training? When they got out of the boxes to actually run, well, does brain meltdown mean anything?

At this point in time the less said about some of these things, the better. Maybe a little later on, Betty and David will regale us with hilarious tales, or maybe not.

Ok...Ok...Maybe just a quick one or two...

I stood on the porch of the cabin and watched as Betty and David drove the first two teams in from the place where the truck and trailer were disabled.

 Betty drove a team of the old timers from their original freight team. Her favorite, Wrangell ran double lead with (I think) Seal. I'm pretty sure Talker and Ando were in wheel. Later Betty told me that Seal was a bit put out because he likes to run double lead with his twin brother. Betty had chosen to put Wrangell up there instead because that was where he usually always ran. This was her first time sledding a team through the Alaskan wilderness. It was natural for her to put the dog in whom she had the most confidence up front automatically. It was really not that big a deal. Seal just pouted a little while the next day. He cheered right up when David and Betty rearranged the dog yard and his brother was next to him.

David drove in a team of the youngsters led by his faithful Aurora. This would not be her only run in. He drove the sled that Col. Vaughan allowed him to use. It was thick and heavy and well-built. By the standards of the sleds I was used to looking at in the lower 48, this solid vehicle with a bed over

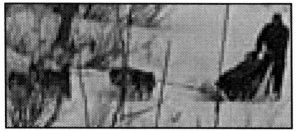 6 feet long was humongous. Somehow it looked just right behind 6 vigorous malamutes.

Once they had the first 10 dogs settled on their chains, Carolyn towed them on the sleds behind her snow machine, back out to the truck for another group.

What with the trips out to the big truck for supplies (earlier) and us in the cabin trying to get some things settled in and put away, I think I missed the middle group of dogs coming in. I did see Carolyn come in once with little baby Bubba (Kotzebue) draped across the seat of the snow machine in front of her. Bub seemed quite content to get a ride and equally happy to greet her friends when she was placed on her chain in the dog yard.

The light was fading fast. No, it was pretty well gone by the time David came in with yet another team. Betty was not right behind him. She came in a little later. I will try to recount some bits and pieces of how things went on that last trip.

There was some confusion in getting away from the trucks. Betty had her weight pullers in front of the sled and Tundra in it. She wouldn't ask him to try to keep up with anyone else over unfamiliar territory, in the dark. Carolyn was having trouble finding David. He had yet another young team and had brought Aurora out with him to guide them in. Carolyn was calling for David and kept slowing down looking for him. (Understand that the noise of the snow machine added to the confusion of the moment.) Once Rory got "her" team straightened out and going fairly smoothly, she found the snow machine rather a nuisance as it kept getting in her way. She knew she was supposed to head up the trail to the cabin. So she cut off the trail through the woods and came out in front of Carolyn and her machine. She was cruising along pretty well by the time Carolyn found out and hurried up to help guide them in.

Betty and her weight pullers had been slow getting going for several reasons and were soon left behind. Betty was aware that neither she nor her team knew the way from there so once the others got out of sight she just stopped and waited for them to come back for her. So there sat Betty with Eskiemo and Chena in front of her sled and Tundra in the basket, in the darkness, in the woods, in Alaska, alone...

Then she heard a sound. Very softly at first, then with growing volume and insistence. It was Tundra growling. About the time Betty realized this and followed his gaze into the darkness, she became aware that the growls had multiplied. Now it was threefold. She drew her gaze from seeing nothing in the darkness, back to her dogs. All of them were staring in the exact same direction. That was enough for her!

Betty swiftly snapped Chena in lead and told her, "Take Momma home!" ("Home" has always been the dog truck when they were on the road.) The big dogs happily hit their harnesses and moved out. They were back at the truck (a mile plus in distance) in what seemed like minutes. Betty knew that if they needed safety, they could all just climb in.

That's where Carolyn and David found them...much to their surprise.

The important thing is that by the end of the evening all of the dogs were safely staked out in front of the cabin. Col. Vaughan had allowed them to use one of his old freight sleds. The things we call freight sleds down in the lower 48 are mere peanuts compared to that beauty. (ok...call it runner envy) With that and the sled that they had brought along, David and Betty made several runs in from the truck to bring the dogs to the cabin.

Throughout all of this day, Carolyn and her snow machine were on the go constantly making it possible to get this much done. David and Betty were totally unfamiliar with this territory and they had been traveling cross-country, not on actual discernible trails. They needed to follow Carolyn on every trip so they didn't get lost.

Here's an interesting side note. While helping guide in the malamutes that were confined for more than two weeks in dog boxes, Carolyn was often going at speeds of 25 to 27 mph.

The following day was spent trying to decide about some options. The idea of unloading that large equipment truck by dogsled was definitely daunting. The few miles from the large parking lot to the cabin is actually more like ten or so. The box-stale dogs are really not up to that much quite yet. Getting green youngsters to run on totally unfamiliar trails is something to be working toward, not planning on doing this week maybe 100 times or so. Asking the old timers to do it, especially after that long trip, would be totally unfair and unrealistic.

Another item under consideration is the fact that David and Betty will be needing outside jobs also. The lack of accessibility here could be a serious drawback. Carolyn said she knew someone who was looking for a dog handler, a person who does dog tours. Upon telephone contact she said that the malamutes are also very picturesque. It might be possible to use them with the tourists also. The idea sounded good. So did the cabin and dog yard area that were a part of the deal she offered.

Carolyn gave David and Betty a snow machine ride out to their truck to meet with the possible employer. They also needed to make arrangements to repair the damage on the truck so they could pull the dog trailer again.

Douglas and I stayed at the cabin. We filled the water jugs and buckets from the small hand pump next to the footpath outside. Doug did the dishes and later I did some laundry. My camping buddies back in the States would have been proud of me, standing on the porch in Alaska, hand washing a few items. They took all day and most of the night to dry. I made a venison pot roast with buttered potatoes and mushrooms for supper on the oil stove that was used for heating the cabin. When we finally ate supper, I served of a side order my own camping specialty, orange smiles.

David and Betty didn't get back until after 10:00 in the evening. They have made arrangements with someone for David to go and weld the truck. That was one good thing. But the job offer that had sounded so good, fell through. It seems that somewhere between the time of the phone call and the actual interview, that the terms of the job offer had changed drastically. Something we have all noticed lately is that often people will say one thing and then change it totally. At first we thought that seemed like an Alaskan foible, perhaps because here we feel more dependent on what we are told. However, considering all the things that have been problems for this endeavor so far, from people not fulfilling promises to help prepare for this trip, to the serious discrepancies about the rental truck and several other things beyond that, I guess that tendency is more widespread than we would like to believe. A little disappointing in human nature, I guess.

OK, now we are finally up to today, Friday, December 28.

David and Betty have gone into town again. Carolyn sent a man over to for David and Betty to hire to give them a ride with his snow machine... at least as far as where the dog truck is parked. They will go into Trapper Creek where David has made arrangements to use the tools that he will need to make repairs on the truck. While he is doing that Betty will do a little wash at the laundromat. Then the two of them will check on other cabin possibilities.

Needless to say, Doug and I stayed behind.

Last night David and Betty brought in some more things from the truck, including this notebook so I can do some writing. They also talked about and used the Vaughan bath house. Sometimes they referred to it as the sauna. They suggest that we give it a try today.

The cabin in which we are staying is what Col. Vaughan refers to as his dog handler's cabin. It is a simple affair, obviously built just for practicality. It has wallboard inside walls and outside walls made of slab wood. There are lean-to's running the length of the building on both the north and the south sides. They allow for fairly much outside storage. Good thing because the entire interior of the cabin must measure 10' by 12'.

Cooking is done on either the oil burning heating furnace (maybe 2' x 2', maybe not) or on an iron frame that has two gas burners. Propane fuels the burners as well as the 3 gas lamps that are wall mounted. The decor (?) is very practical. A bed, a loft, a set of shelves, a long counter with cabinets to serve as kitchen and work bench, hooks and pegs on the walls make up our basic living area. The only decorations are a picture of a Siberian husky on one wall and a wall hanging of what is presumably a wolf on another. Reasonable and serviceable.

The Vaughan's own cabin is very nice! Actually constructed of logs nearly a foot in diameter, it is solid and impressive. The interior is decorated with all kinds of things that are actually used in this part of the world. Mostly ski and dog equipment.

I will tell you about the decorations in one small building. As you walk in the door there is a picture window to your right. Over it hang a dog whip and a fishing pole. The wall in front of you holds a snow hook and a full-siwash style harness. On the wall to the left hang two sets of ice cleats that can be strapped onto boots for traction when the weather demands so. There is also a pair of snowshoes. The wall holding the door in which you have just come also holds a canvas piece with handles for toting in wood and an old fashioned washboard. That is the outhouse.

After a breakfast of leftover venison made into stew, David and Betty had gone. Doug and I filled the water and then did some other odd jobs around the cabin. Then I walked over and located the sauna.

It was well made and really rather nice. I fired it up and while it was heating walked back to the cabin for clean clothes and things. By the time I came back the wood fire had melted the ice in the cauldron back to water. The rocks around that were getting nice and hot. I took a little sauna, a clean snow face-wash, had a hand shower with the nice warm water, and then sauna-ed a little more. I figured that I must have been there about ten to fifteen minutes. I felt great coming out! It's a part of the Alaskan experience! Embrace it!! (Don't worry, Mom. I wasn't naked in the Alaskan wilderness. I kept my hat on the whole time!)

As I said, I estimated about ten or fifteen minutes for that. Amazingly, Douglas seems to have done about an hour's worth of cleanup, dishes and other things. Maybe I was in there a little longer than I had thought.

Douglas went next. After that we built up the fire and banked it and left it burning so David and Betty could have a real sauna when they get back, if they return fairly early.

I watched the dogs as they played in the dog yard. In comparison to their old life, a 12 ft. circle doesn't seem like much. However, in comparison to spending over two weeks in dog boxes, this must seem like Heaven. They are having so much fun, digging in the snow for treasure, pulling up sticks and stumps of scrub bushes and trees that had been cut down to form the dog yard. They occupy their time chewing up their new found treasures and playing with each other and sometimes just rolling around in the bright snow. This is good for them. When the time comes to get back to work, they will be more ready.

David and Betty got back to the cabin late. 11:00 PM. David has the truck welded but they found no new place to stay. Since we drove out of the driveway in Michigan, no before that, even before I drove the rental truck out of the driveway in Illinois, their money has been dwindling rapidly. Of course both of them are troubled by this.

Also while they were in town, people mentioned problems with moose and bears, and that was in areas not nearly this remote. Betty was worried about it. Of course David, like any red-blooded American man, had to tease her about it. You know, the usual, first chuckling about it, then later looking out a window or door and gasping. By the time we were all ready to go to bed, Betty was telling David that she was not amused. While they were in town they had made some phone calls for me. Betty phoned my mom to tell her everything was OK and that I was out in a cabin in the woods. They also tried the airlines, or maybe they tried to go through the area travel agency. Apparently everything up here is shut down for the holidays so there is no flight for me very soon. That is disappointing.

David was tired and went to bed. Betty stayed up and talked with me for awhile. She told me about a man (maybe native American) who talked with her in the bar while David worked on the truck in the garage behind. When she started to talk about the dogs, he already seemed to know everything she was going to tell him. They were up here with malamutes. They want to run the Iditarod. They don't expect to win. They just want to show that malamutes can do it. Betty said, "Word sure gets around up here!"

Betty and Kotzubue

While we were talking, the dogs began to make a lot of racket. They were all looking the same way, into the woods. Betty hollered for David to wake up and load a gun just in case. He came down from the loft with one, ready for action. He opened the door and the rest of us watched out the window. That was when about three or four snow machines buzzed out of the woods and across the clearing beyond the dog yard and back into the woods. We all had a good laugh. It sure helped to break the tension. "How many points for a snowmobiler if you bag them on the run?"

David went back to bed. Betty and I continued talking. Suddenly there was more ruckus from the dogs...really a lot this time. We looked out the window and could see what the problem was. There was a dog running loose in the dog yard! At first we were afraid it was a stranger. It turned out to be sweet little Taylor. She came running to the cabin when we opened the door and called her. Poor David was up again, of course. It turned out, in the confusion of mushing all the dogs in the other day, somebody must have snapped a neckline onto her tie out chain instead of taking it off. Taylor had chewed through it and gone romping. She got a brief petting for coming when called and for not running off, although we are sure that she had no intentions of leaving. Then David pulled his boots on and walked her back down to her place in the dog yard. After that, everybody settled down and we all got some sleep.

Saturday December 29, 2001

David was up early and has gone to move the dog trailer before it gets snowed in. Betty is out cleaning in the dog yard. She is doing more than cleaning. She takes the time to pet and go over each dog. She runs her hands over them. She is checking for condition, attitude and weight. She is doing a little grooming too, stripping the dead hair that they are blowing, out of their coats to allow new to grow in. These are not only chores that need to be done. Betty is in her element. This is home to her. Her dogs are her home. She takes the time to touch each one, to touch base, to reconnect. As I watch her move from one to the other it looks as though they are refilling her, with hope... with their strength... with their love. She takes it in. It seems to flow through her as she returns it to them. It has multiplied. Now there is enough for her and for them.

This trip has been hard on her. She has expended huge amounts of energy, physical and emotional. This has been true for all of us, but by far, mostly for her. She has never wavered in her faith or her love. In this time with the dogs they are drawing from and giving to each other.

It is not all sweet and ethereal however. After all she is

out there with a shovel. And she is working, really working. The cleaning part of the task is taking longer than it should because as the dogs dig through the snow to the ground, they are uncovering feces left over from previous dogs. Betty is cleaning it up, saying, "I don't want my dogs to lay in sh___ !" And "I don't want to pet my dogs and have my hands smell like an outhouse!"

This is a good time to stick in my little insert on headwear... so here goes.

When I was young I never wore a hat of any kind. I disliked them intensely. Since I have gotten into dogsledding I have discovered that some form of headwear is absolutely necessary. I have also discovered that living with and observing everybody's headwear can be a lot of fun. Here is an article that I wrote that talks a little bit about a much bigger subject that I have been observing for years. Even though it's true... it is fun.

Dogsledding with Ivan and Elmer

When I was young, I never wore a hat. I had no use for them. When I became a dogsledder I realized that they were a necessary part of my equipment.

There are all kinds of hats. It seems that dogsledders need to find the right hat for them. If you are going to wear something on your head for days and days, it needs to be something that you are comfortable with. Strangely enough your hat, like your dogs and your sled, becomes not only your friend but an extension of yourself.

When I go to dog events, I look at all the people there and I see how each person's hat is a part of their personality. Sometimes this is intentional. Sometimes is just happens.

Some people, men especially, seem to like to wear dead animals on their heads. It is very common to be able to easily identify various species perched on top of various heads. If an outsider is trying to find someone it is fairly easy to direct them with a phrase like, "that tall guy over there with the beaver on his head."

But there is a much greater variety to see. Warmth of course is the deciding factor. The hat must do its job of keeping its wearer snug and dry.

My good friend and dogsledding buddy, Delores, proudly wears a hat that was formerly worn by a Russian soldier. When the Berlin wall came down, and when the Soviet Union separated, relations with people of other countries changed, became more open. Well, I don't think that I will go into it any more... that's Delores' tale to tell. Suffice to say that my friend wears a very unique hat. She enjoys the story. She enjoys the look of the hat. It keeps her head warm. And in blustery weather the ear flaps fasten under her chin to keep her ears warm and to keep the thing from blowing away. She calls it Ivan.

For many years I wore whatever I grabbed out of the drawer full of winter wear kept at my house. I dislike knit caps because they always creep up on my head. I either lose them or I wind up looking like somebody's demented uncle. Not very flattering. On the rare occasions I get one that fits me correctly, eventually it becomes misplaced, snitched by someone else, or washed and shrunk.

Then one day, my sister brought me a filled nylon hat. It was ugly! It had flaps that fastened on top of it with velcro. It looked remarkably like the hat that Elmer Fudd always has on his head while he is hunting Bugs Bunny. To make it even uglier, the color was blaze orange. I took it so as not to hurt my sister's feelings. I tossed it behind the seat of my pickup truck. For about a year I forgot it was there. Then one cold blustery day a group of us were going out dogsledding. While we were setting up, the wind was raw. I could not find whatever hat it was that I had been wearing. I considered just doing without. That wind was harsh. We were planning to go through a lot of open territory. I looked in my truck to see if I could come up with something to do the job. That was when I came across that ugly orange hat. Oh well, at least my companions would be able to see me. I slapped that on top of my head. Off we went across the countryside. At least it was big enough. Before dark the wind picked up and became even sharper. I wished that it was big enough to cover my ears. Then I remembered the Velcro flaps. I pulled them apart and down over my cold ears. Then I realized that the Velcro would refasten underneath my chin. I had a friend.

I have a friend. His name is Elmer. He is still ugly, but we work well together.

When I drove up to Alaska with David and Betty and Doug and the rest of the dream team, I had the opportunity to observe their headwear. Betty usually wears a thick headband.

It covers her ears and keeps her head fairly warm. But when the weather gets colder she needs more protection. She showed me some hats that she had fixed to suit her needs. They were hats that had ear flaps and a short bill. I think they were wool. She showed me how she sewed ribbons on to the bottom of each ear flap. That way she could tie them under her chin. Doing it that way kept her head warmer and prevented the whole thing from blowing off even in a very high wind or on a very fast dogsled.

David's headwear is even more interesting. I am pretty sure it is, or at least was manufactured by the United States government, probably the army. I say that because it is army green. I suppose it could have been manufactured by the air corps.

If Elmer is remindful of a cartoon character, I must admit that I would name David's headwear, Snoopy. The hat that seems to be his favorite to wear looks for all the world just like the one that Snoopy wears when he is fighting the Red Baron.

Now our friend Douglas who drove up with us, seems to have two favorites. I suppose he likes the color blue. One of his hats is a good sturdy blue wool hat. It has a bill out front like a baseball cap and has good sturdy ear flaps that hang down. It is a good serviceable hat. He has another hat that is more of a challenge to describe. It is also blue and probably woolen. It seems to be made from a lot of fabric. When he puts it on his head it sort of wraps around and extends upward. In the cartoon character department. I am slightly torn between Marge Simpson and a Smurf. The Smurf wins... hands down.

While she was a taking care of the dogs, Betty worked out the plan to rearrange the dogs to a more efficient system. She has moved several of them already during the day and plans for her and David to move the rest of them tonight after supper.

While she was working she found a bucket with meat that had been left near the dog yard. Something had taken some of the meat and run off in the direction of a nearby shed. The tracks were not very big but they were also not very clear. We wondered if it had been a wild animal or just a stray dog. In either case it didn't seem good. We didn't like to think of a wild animal that bold. And we weren't too crazy about stray dogs either. David and Betty's dogs have never been allowed to fight and they certainly didn't want a stranger to teach them to. There was also the consideration of the females coming into heat whenever they happened to, whether it was the correct time or not. (Oh, did I mention that that was one of the primary reasons for the brain meltdown when the dogs finally got out of the dog truck?)

(We have since learned that heat cycles are one of the things that are a little goofy for sled dogs in training. When human women, long distance runners, are in vigorous train-

ing, very often they stop having their menstrual cycles alto-gether. It is not necessarily universal, but it is certainly not uncommon. With the canine female athletes, just the oppo-site seems to be true. They pop into heat season whenever they seem to feel like it. Of course as an added bonus, usu-ally one coming in brings everybody or nearly everybody else in too. One of the things to work on in training is to ignore such things when in harness. There are plenty of humorous tales about different methods people have tried to use to combat this problem.)

Late this afternoon, Betty decided to climb the hill behind the cabin to see what was up there. From the top she could see Denali, the highest mountain peak on the North American continent, otherwise known as Mt. McKinley. While she was up there looking around, she said she found some large tracks in the snow. I was standing on the porch, about 50 yards downhill from her. When she called down to me about the large tracks, I suggested, "David ?" Thinking that he had made them to tease her some more.

She replied, "No, they don't come from that direction."

I called up the hill to her, "The only way to tell where they do come from is to follow them and I don't think that is a good idea this time of day."

I heard a distant muffled," No!"

And then, Betty was standing beside me!

"A moose made the tracks!"

"How could you tell ?"

"It's there now!!"

Later this evening, as we were telling David about it, Betty was wondering out loud which animal it was that can run downhill and which one can't. One is a bear and one is a moose. We recall, (at least legend has it) that the moose can-not run down hill because its long legs have trouble with coor-dination. The bear, however, can run downhill like a locomo-tive. So I told David, "Now I know two things that can run downhill, a bear, and your wife!"

David and Betty are discussing plans to get the dogs back to working. It is surprising how much snow machine traffic there is around here. While they were in town, some of the locals have told Betty and David that this is no longer the area for working dogs that it used to be. The snow machine traffic makes it dangerous, especially on the weekends. And the snow machines themselves make moguls all over the trails. They are unbelievably hard on people's equipment and teams. Basically the plan for now is to do very short training runs right out in front of the dog yard, in the large clearing that we can see from that cabin, on the weekends. During the week is when the longer trips will have to be. At least for starters.

We talked about using the sauna. It does use up firewood. Col. Vaughan ordered some firewood to be dropped off. Instead of dumping it near the cabin, whoever brought it dumped it at the top of the driveway. In order to use it we would have to haul it all the way down the hill and stack it in lean-to next to the sauna.

David plans to hire someone tomorrow to go out to the truck and bring in barrels for the dogs to sleep in. The weather has been good so far and the dogs are completely enjoying sleeping stretched out in the snow. We need to be prepared when the weather changes.

Sunday, December 30, 2001

David and Betty are out in the dog yard working. Two guys on a snow machine pull up and stop to visit. One of them is an experienced dog racer and the other one is something like his apprentice. They came over to look at the malamutes. They also stop by to tell David and Betty that they need to move the dog truck before it gets snowed in. David has been parking it in the clearing where they dropped the dogs on Christmas night. The visitors tell him if the truck gets snowed in, David will not be able to make it to any races this season. "There are a lot of people that would like that." Hmmmmm... The men offer to give David a lift on their snow machine so he can go out to move it, but just then, the snow machine that he hired shows up. Betty visits with the people a little longer as David goes out to the trucks.

Apparently everybody up here knows what is going on, even when they pretend not to. We were only up here a few days and Betty and David were explaining to almost everyone they met, "No, we don't want Alaskan huskies. Yes, we will run our own dogs. No, we don't expect to win. We are just up here to prove that Malamutes can do this... etc.etc.etc."

Since most dogsledders up here are racers, they pretty universally run the fast, small, light mixed breeds. They have a sincere difficulty even trying to understand why anyone would want to run in races for any reason but winning. The entire concept of even caring about purebreds or keeping them pure or doing something 'for the breed' seems to be a total mystery to most of the people that we have encountered. Actually we have not met very many people here that are familiar with the malamute breed. They do seem to comprehend that they are something from the past. They virtually never call them by their breed name. They just call them "the Big Dogs".

After the visitors have gone Betty continues to work in the dog yard. When a load of barrels comes in from the truck she goes about settling them into the snow in strategic places for the dogs to use. Before long David returns with a second load of barrels and other equipment from the big truck. Time is spent putting things away in the cabin. David and Betty finish placing the dog barrels that are here and some wooden dog houses that the Vaughans have allowed them to use.

I enjoy watching the dogs interact. Betty and David have adjusted the chains so each dog can play with the dogs around it but the chains can't cross and cause a tangle. The only exceptions are when someone's heat cycle demands a shorter chain temporarily. They have placed Aurora and Bubba next to each other because they have always been each other's special playmate.

All of the dogs spend some time playing and interacting with each other. This is good for morale and positive socialization that will be valuable on the trail.

They do have a pack order but with David and Betty as strong alphas there is no serious vying for promotion. There is a strong feeling of respect among the younger dogs toward the older ones though. They seem to covet their attention and defer to their authority. They are like a group of children that have been raised by venerable aunts and uncles.

Ando seems to be the crusty old uncle every puts up with and loves. He has definitely been marked by his early years of hardship. He is distinctly grumpy. He growls. When it is directed towards other dogs it seems to say, "Behave yourself. Don't bug me. Toe the mark". When directed occasionally toward people, there is really no threat to it. It is obvious in his tone and his posture. It is more like, "Don't pick on me" and "I really don't need to put up with this."

Ando is surrounded by Seal and Talker and Q.T. and Taylor. The three old timers just seem to get along in a companionable way, like old guys on a park bench. The two young girls sometimes approach the old fellow. When Q.T. does, she just walks over near him. If he waves his tail, the two of them stand near as if pleasantly visiting. If he grumps at her she just goes over and lies down a little further away. But Taylor is so cute. She approaches him in a submissive manner, head down and tilted to one side, tail wagging low. He invariably grumps at her. Then she really goes into her routine. More wagging, more tilting, even a silly look on her face. He reacts by stiffening and straightening up more. Head high, arrogant posture. She fawns even more. Eyebrows scrunched, licking her lips, her tilting advances to a shoulder tip that advances all the way to a sort of sideways somersault and there she lies upside down extending a paw to him. Throughout all this that tail has never stopped, only increased in speed. Now in its tucked position upside over, it is sticking up in the air behind her almost vibrating. They each hold their respective positions. If Ando is feeling particularly generous he might grace her with a little snarl

snarl and some teeth-baring. Either one of them could walk away at any time. They must stand at the ends of their chains to perform this ritual, and ritual it is. It fulfills a need in both of them. He has the tremendous ego boost of a groveling worshipper. She has the attention of the powerful god-like creature she adores. That's a simplification...but you get the idea.

This might be a good time for a little talk about the weather. (Very little)
We were blessed on the way out with virtually no snow during traveling hours. There were several times that it snowed overnight but it always quit by the time we were ready to go. It was severely cold as we traveled through very much of Canada. Probably most of the time it was below zero degrees Fahrenheit. Nights that we spent in the Canadian Rockies the temperature was around -28 or -36 degrees Fahrenheit. Once it was even -44 degrees Fahrenheit. Actually people that we talked to said that when it came down to that far below zero, they didn't even pay attention to whether it was Fahrenheit or Celsius because when it was so cold there wasn't that much difference between them.

It seemed as though the weather softened as we approached the Alaskan border. As we arrived here the temperatures were above zero. Now they are hovering somewhere around 20 degrees Fahrenheit. Nice! Since we have been in the cabin we have usually gotten a little bit of overnight snowfall. It has always been light and fluffy and never more than 2 inches of it at a time. So far....

I was just out on the porch trying to film Betty working in the dog yard. I was wearing a flannel shirt over my T-shirt and my trusty rusty Elmer Fudd hat. I was warm and comfortable with that much on to stand there and film for about ten minutes.

Before we go to sleep at night... we place a whole frozen turkey in a huge kettle with some water on top of the heating stove.

Monday December 31, 2001
New Year's Eve!

We got up pretty early this morning. The sunrise was very red. We watched the day dawn over the mountain range that we could see up in the distance from the front of the cabin. I believe they are the Talkeetna's. The colors in the sky are very beautiful but are they a signal of upcoming rough weather? There are clouds in the sky above this beautiful sunrise. There are clouds off and on, pretty much all of the time.

After breakfast we brought some dogs in for a nail trimming and foot care session. I tried to document quite a bit of that on film.

David took out some small teams for practice work. To the eager dogs, this was a play fun time. It is a chance to get off of their chains and out of the dog yard. It is also a chance for important exercise and command training time. But the dogs just think that they are having fun!

Aurora is so far clearly the best lead dog of the young team. David was in a hurry to get some teams on the trail and get working but there was so much to do before he got to it that he was really pretty fired up to go. He finally stepped onto the runners and called out happily, "Hike! Hike it! Gee!" immediately followed by "Oh, sh__"

Aurora exuberantly swung her team off the trail that they had started down and aimed them through chest deep snow toward the one that led to the right. With David's expletive she stopped in her tracks, team and all, and looked over her shoulder at him.

He said, "I'm sorry Aurora, I meant Haw!"

With a cheerful wave of her tail, as if to say, "I thought so!", she swung the entire team nearly 180 degrees in the deep snow and in seconds reached the trail originally intended. They all raced gleefully out of sight. I find a lot of Aurora's appeal to be not only the power, accuracy and control she has of her team but the pure joy she exhibits when responding to David's every command, and even his extra thoughts. (the Oh,Sh... for example). If everyone could see and feel this kind of joy, bad would probably be forced to just vanish from the world.

Betty takes Eskiemo alone and hauls down some of the wood that was left at the top of the driveway. They don't bring all of it down because the plastic sled she is using keeps trying to hit Eskiemo. She tried using a dog sled behind him to haul it down, but it only has a padbreak and is very unwieldy. It keeps going off to the side and tries to tip over. She hauls enough, however, for us to be able to start the sauna and be able to use it this evening. But first, that turkey in the kettle spends some time on top of the wood fire.

Later we have a complete turkey dinner with mashed potatoes, sweet potatoes, green beans, and turkey dressing. We even have canned peaches for dessert. It is a real holiday meal!

Then everybody gets the chance to take a sauna and a bath. We are all finished, back in the cabin and lying in our respective bunks by 11:40 PM. I announce to everybody that we have to stay awake for 20 more minutes. Someone asks, "What for ?" I reply. "The new year."

That is the last that I remember, but even so, I may have been the last one asleep.

Tuesday, January 1, 2002
HAPPY NEW YEAR!!

We all slept in a bit. When I arise David is already heading out to take care of the dogs. He says to be quiet and allow Betty to get some more sleep. I work in the kitchen for awhile. As I watch him out the window, I observe the same care and love and attention that I was seeing the other day as I watched Betty. Now that I think about it, I realize that it looks so familiar because I have been watching it all the way out here.

Betty awakens and complains that she should be doing the dog yard so David can work small teams. I remind her that its New Year's Day. The snowmobile traffic will be heavy very

soon. Besides David needs to do this with the dogs too. As she watches him out the window, lying up there in the loft, there is no doubt in my mind that she knows exactly what I mean. She allows herself to doze off. That extra bit of sleep is very good for her.

Later on we all have fruit pancakes and bacon for breakfast. We do some more nail trimming and foot care. Then there seems to be a gap in the traffic with the snow machines. David takes advantage of it to do some more close by command training with small teams.

Coming back from one of the short trips, David is driving a three-dog team. Funny, I could have sworn he left with four dogs. As he is pulling up alongside the dog yard, I notice a movement through the trees. Something is coming Hell-for-leather, down the trail behind him. As he steps off the runners and sets his snow hook, it bursts upon him in a flurry of the snow. The "it" is Gateway. David catches him and walks him back to his tie-out in the dog yard. Then he goes about his business of putting away the team and taking another one out to work.

Betty is also down the hill, I have to wait until they are both finished with what they're doing before I get an explanation. It is this...

In the excitement of running, Gateway committed an unacceptable act. He was so excited that he bit the dog next to him. He wasn't actually trying to start a fight, it was just an expression of excitement? Enthusiasm? No, I guess pure foolishness. Well, the punishment for fighting, after being scruffed, scolded and may be even an ear bite, is to lose the privilege of running with the team. David had taken Gateway off the team and tied him to a tree next to the trail. He planned to return for him after he put the team way. However, he had tied Gateway with a leash that he happened to have on the sled. He was only about a quarter of a mile from the dog yard. He would have been perfectly safe. Gateway did not want to be abandoned! He chewed through the leash and did his very best to try to rejoin his team.

I manage a telephone call home. Then I try the airlines. The most practical flight out is one week from today. I make a tentative reservation. I have 48 hours to confirm that or I will lose it. At this point, the main question is if I can get to the airport at that time. Right now it seems that the plan is to dog sled out to someone with a snow machine and get a ride to that 4 wheel drive truck to drive to the highway to get to Anchorage.

When the snow machine traffic outside picked up again, David finished working with the small teams. Then he and Betty repaired the steps outside. Then they re-situated Tundra and Dehlia to create a space for Nanook and her upcoming Idita-puppies.

Wednesday, January 2, 2002

Another day of working here at the cabin. We continue to do nail trimming and foot care. With 30 dogs to do it takes quite a while to work our way through each and every one of them. Now that the holiday is pretty well past, Betty and David decide to take team out on the trail/road. They have decided to run a team all the way to the big parking lot and bring in some more of our supplies.

In the evening once they have returned, it is a nice time for talking and visiting. Betty tells me that while they were on the road/trail they happened across Vern Halter, a well-known racer, putting his dogs away after a practice. He watched them work and said to Betty, "Hmm, pretty slow, eh?"
Betty retorted, "You would be slow too if you were a ten year old weightpull dog!"

She was referring to big silver gray Chena, their lead dog for that trip.

Then he said, "Oh! Pretty fast!".

One of the things that I can do around here is to cook. I didn't bring any real winter clothes because I had planned on a 6-day drive and then walking from the truck to an airplane. The only boots I have are the kind that stop about an inch below my ankles. Considering that the snow here anyplace off the regular paths is about fanny deep, I am very limited in what I can do outside. Ok, so I cook.

Today I made soup with the broth from cooking the turkey, and everything else I could find to put into it. I felt that I made a nice hearty soup with lots of meat and vegetables. When David and Betty came in for supper they seemed to welcome the nice hot meal. In general we had only two rules about cooking. No cheese in the overall makings. (David really hates it. The rest of us can add it to our own portions but to put it into the general pot would be unfair because then he wouldn't eat it. We all know that he is the biggest eater and legitimately so because he burns the calories like there's no tomorrow. So it is no big deal. We can each add it to our own when we want it.) The other rule sort of ties in with that. It is that each of us can add anything we want to our own portion to make it different, spicier, blander, sweeter, more sour, anything we want. Anyway, everybody adds crackers to their soup don't they?
Well, David tastes the soup and says he really likes it. Then he goes about adding his own touch. By the time he finishes

adding about everything in the kitchen except his boots, his bowl of 'soup' stands about an inch over the top rim of his bowl. I can't resist. I find a camera and take a picture of it.

Ribbing going on here??

Nooooo, not much.

David talked a little bit about Tundra. He said that Tundra's heritage goes back to the World War II dogs that carried ammunition and supplies for the United States army. The man that they bought Tundra from trained dogs to parachute out of airplanes to do their jobs. Tundra's relatives were included in that group of dogs.

Once, when David and Betty were running the team near Dollar Bay in Michigan's upper peninsula, they were running at night. David had run these trails a few times before. Tundra was his lead dog for those runs. Well, he was his lead dog on this run also. Suddenly he stopped the whole team and refused to continue on the trail. David tried to get him to go but he was adamant. Finally David had to allow him to go off trail to pass whatever was bothering him. As they approached the area Tundra refused to go to, David could see a large shape moving in a strange sort of unmoving way. As the dog team went past, David had to shine his light on it. It was revealed to be a large garbage bag partially frozen in the ice and snow, being rattled and wiggled by the wind. David and Betty both laughed at the idea of being afraid of a garbage bag, but Tundra wasn't sure what it was. He knew it was something that did not belong there.

It was sort of a pleasant evening. As we talked David worked on the lines for his sled. Betty also worked on lines, but they were lines of writing. She was working to give me a little resume of each dog on the team.

Thursday, January 3, 2002.

David and Doug went to town today. They had to leave early. David hired someone with a snow machine to take them to the truck. They left the cabin at 9:00 AM. It was not light outside yet.

Tundra's house is right next to the steps for the porch. It is just inside the lean-to so he can be in the house or behind it in the lean-to or lying in the snow just outside. The outside position seems to be his favorite when he sun is out. His dense coat is like a blanket to lie on that can't get rumpled up or be rolled off of. Stretched out soaking up the rays, he looks just like the sunbathers on Daytona Beach.

As I walk past his house this morning, I notice a fairly large Teddy bear sitting just inside his doghouse. I have to look

twice because it is the same color as Tundra. At first I thought I was having a weird sort of double-vision attack. There he was sun-bathing, no, he's there in the house, no. Well I hadn't noticed that bear before.

After Betty was done with her work in the dog yard, she brought QT up to the cabin. Betty trimmed QT's nails and put a harness on her. Then the two of them went up the driveway to haul firewood back down. They made several trips. Betty was giving her special attention. As a youngster she had shown great promise. Lately she seems to be having some kind of an attitude problem. Betty hopes that with work and a little special attention QT can regain the promise of her past.

When she was done with her outside work, Betty sat down and made up some pills for Wrangell. She has several different herbal remedies which are formulas she has devised herself. These formulas are getting very good results. Her beautiful lead dog Wrangell has had a strange malady (H. Pyloric?) that is usually fatal to its victim within a year. Apparently it is usually treated with antibiotics but they often have a pretty devastating effect due to the concentration required. Wrangell got it in 1996. Instead of succumbing to it years ago, he is still going strong. The same formula has enjoyed success for human use also. Betty also makes a natural formula to relieve the pain and symptoms of gout. A little while before she left for Alaska, someone called and asked if she would leave him enough remedy to serve him in case he develops problems while she is gone. This was in very late fall/early winter. She usually grows or gathers her own herbs that comprise the remedies that she creates. So there she was, out in the field brushing snow off of plants to gather enough to make a large batch to tide him over until she returns. It took five hours to bring in enough because the plants were not growing that time of year and all of the leaves were tiny. She has several other natural formulas. She would like to be able to make these available to other people but she does not want formulas stolen. She has had dog food formulas stolen and put into commercial use more than once. The results have been very good for the company that did it, and for its customers and their pets. But she has never gotten any financial remuneration for it. She would not like the same sort of thing to happen with her natural formulas. I suggested that she patent them and then try to market them. She said that she would like to, but needs to find out the correct way to do it. Right now she is a little busy. I guess that's one thing she will have to put on hold for awhile.

While she is making up the capsules, I mention Tundra's Teddy. She tells me that she brought it in from the truck for him yesterday. It means a lot to him. (Oh, sure...) I think there is nothing that these people (no, this family) say or do that doesn't have a story or a reason behind it. The Teddy bear used to belong to Suntrana, the first Suntrana, the one that the present one is named after. She was Tundra's mate. The teddy was her toy. She played with it, carried it around and slept with it. After she passed away Betty put it up on a shelf. Tundra, like David and Betty, mourned their loss. Sometimes Betty would see Tundra just sitting. He seemed to be staring off into space. This went on for weeks. Then Betty noticed a pattern to the behavior. Wherever he was sitting when he was staring, his gaze was actually pointing at the same spot in the house, the shelf where Suntrana's bear reposed. So, of course, Betty asked him if he wanted it. He walked to the shelf and stood wagging his tail slowly. She gave it to him and he has had it ever since. Automatically, I glance out the door toward him. The sun has gone. The bear has fallen out of the house. Tundra lies just inside the leanto with one paw on the bear.

The guys finally got back between nine and 10:00 PM. They brought a bucket of chicken, a cell phone, and an airplane ticket for me! About time!! (I am a little put out because I could have flown out of Anchorage on the seventh of January if I could have confirmed the reservation I tried to make days ago. Now I have to wait until the 10th. As wonderful as this adventure is, it has taken many times longer than we had planned. The terrific people that are caring for my home and animals were not asked to do it for this long. I feel that I am imposing on them unfairly.)

While they were out the men also bought some plywood to build a whelping box for Nanook. They couldn't carry it here on a snow machine so they left it at the truck for now. Before we all went to sleep David and Betty did Kotzebue's nails and foot care.

Friday, January 4, 2002

David and Betty dogsled to the truck to bring in the plywood. They left after taking care of morning chores, so they didn't actually get on the trail until 1:20 PM. It is about a 20 miles round trip. Aurora is their leader, running double with Iditarod. The rest of the team is composed of Coleen, Taylor, Alaska, and Brook. (I think...)
Douglas and I stayed at the cabin. Doug walked Dehlia,

cleaned up after her, and burned the garbage. I made spaghetti sauce. Then I walked over and stacked the wood for the sauna that I had said I would. Even though I am "pouting" about the late departure date. I still did what I had said that I would do. If your word is only as good as your mood, it is really worth nothing! I am not that way.

I telephone home. Robin says the puppies are adorable. I knew they would be. She says that she brings them down stairs for socialization with their grandmothers, one at a time. Each of the grandmothers want to protect the puppies from the other. So it is the grandmothers that are one at a time. All the puppies come downstairs. Mom is surprised by the late travel date but will make arrangements for someone to pick me up at O'Hare field in Chicago.

It snowed all day yesterday. It is snowing all day today. The snowfall is light and fluffy. Today we cannot even see to the Talkeetna Range, the mountains straight across from the cabin that we can usually view out the window.

David and Betty return to the cabin about 6:20 PM. They have been gone about five hours. They gave the dogs a one hour rest in the parking lot. They also took time to load the sled with various supplies and the large awkward sheets of the plywood. I cannot imagine trying to load a 4 ft. by 6 ft. sheet of plywood onto a dogsled. Trying to drive down a trail, especially a rough one, certainly must be impossible. However, David and Betty have brought in several sheets. Betty tells

me they would have been back much sooner, but they kept getting stopped by admirers on snow machines. She says that one guy looked at the load they were carrying and you could see him counting dogs as he went by. Considering that load, no wonder! Betty says she thinks that they carried more than anybody we have hired with a snow machine and trailer.

The new cell phone is turned on tonight at 10:00 in case of any incoming calls. There are none tonight.

Saturday, January 5, 2002

Yesterday, all day, when David and Betty were gone with the six dog team, the rest of them kept howling and yowling. The dogs in the yard were calling up the trail for them (David, Betty, and the team of six) to hurry back so that they (each of the dogs remaining, meaning to say "I") could have a turn next. It was really something to watch and to hear.

They would all be in full cry for quite awhile. Then suddenly they all stopped. In silence, they would look and listen up the trail. Then one of them (usually Golovin) would begin to call and the rest would all join in again. It went on like that all day.

Today as David starts to work small teams in the clearing in front of the cabin (which we have been told will be a swamp in the springtime), all of the dogs are in full cry. "Pick me! Pick me!" Even the ones that worked so hard and so well yesterday.

As David starts to leave with one of the small teams, he is not 50 yards down the trail when he comes to a sudden halt. He jumps off the runners and sets his snow hook. Then he runs up to the team and grabs one of the wheel dogs. I can see him shake the dog by the ruff. Then he hauls the dog by the scruff of the neck out of the team and over to the trees beside the trail. He leaves the dog there and returns to the sled. Off they go, David and the rest of the team. From the action that has taken place I know without asking this time what has happened. It is also obvious that the dog left jumping up and down next to the tree is Gateway. I hope David had a chain with him this time.

When he returns with the 3-dog team he lavishes praise on them for a good workout. When he then walks up the trail and returns with Gate he doesn't appear to have much to say to him. As he puts him on his chain in the dog yard it looks like he says something to him and gives him a pat of forgiveness.

Today seems to be a day for working out some of the kinks, a tough job with intact males and most of the females in heat. They will get it. There's a little more progress made by the end of each workout. I worry about Gateway.

The rest of the afternoon was spent with David and Betty cutting up the plywood to have the right size pieces in order to build a box/dog house for Nanook to whelp her puppies.

Every evening Tundra and Delia have taken turns to come inside the cabin for a while. Tonight Nanook came in to visit for awhile also. She is a big girl, normally over 90 lbs., but I had not realized how big (in the other sense of the word) she had gotten. She is not only definitely carrying, she is carrying several. Her due date is a little over a week away, maybe nine or ten days.

Sitting in the cabin tonight, David is still working on lines for a bigger team.

Sunday January 6, 2002

The temperatures have been hovering way up around the freezing mark. Today they actually cross it and briefly hover a bit above. Then it rains, not enough to melt the snow or anything, just good for making everything icy.

David and Betty have decided to snowshoe over to a cabin we can see. They have heard that it is for sale or rent. Someone also told them they can use any dog houses from there. They don their snowshoes and head down the hill. They put a long leash on Nanook. She needs some exercise but because of her condition she has not been allowed to run in harness with the teams. Baby Kotzebue hasn't worn harness yet either. So she accompanies them also. She is allowed to run loose and has a ball galloping circles around them and making short runs (mad dashes) ahead, or off to the side and then barreling back to them like a tiny locomotive.

When they come back, they say that the cabin is quite nice. It appears to be quite a bit larger than the one we are living in now. The four of us are presently staying in a cabin that, I believe, measures about ten by twelve feet. They also say that they found only a few very beat up dog houses over there. They would like to acquire wooden doghouses, because most of the dogs want nothing to do with the smooth plastic barrels that we have brought along with us from so far away. It seemed like such a good idea at the time. Maybe if we had a way to scuff up the inside to give them some texture, the dogs would be more tolerant of them. Since they're made of such tough material that task is right now impossible. That is why Betty and David would like to get some of the fussier dogs at least, more common dog houses made of wood. As they talk they decide that perhaps they will go get some and fix them up. They have already done that with some of them that the Vaughans told them they could use from their storage shed.

Most of the afternoon was spent putting together a dog house/whelping box for Nanook. That is a very big job in itself. They are also preparing the leanto and the area around her new home-to-be. They are moving things around and fencing other things off.

Fairly late in the afternoon, the two guys that stopped in to visit before drop in again. They brought with them a beat up version of a dog house. There is a break in the preparations for Nanook to repair the house they brought over. Once it is finished, Artic receives a new home. The two of them do not hang around very long. Before they drive off, the younger one says that he will try to come back over on Tuesday, his half day off.

After they have gone David and Betty make a plywood floor for one of the smooth plastic barrels. The result is a considerable decrease in the interior size of it but that's OK. They have made it for Dehlia. They set it up just south of the cabin. Betty puts on her snowshoes and stamps down a large area in front of it. Then they set Delia her own little dog stake into the ground so she can go into her new house or run around in front of it. They put her out on her new chain, just like the big dogs. She seems to enjoy it. She runs around on her chain.

Then she lies down in the snow and rolls and rolls. She looks just like any child out making snow angels.

Talking this evening David decides to ask our young visitor if he can make arrangements to haul us out to the truck on Wednesday so we can all go to Anchorage and do some shopping and tourist stuff just for the heck of it. Then we will stay overnight in a motel so I can get to the airport early in the morning for my flight home. One last evening together just having fun. We contemplate the idea with relish!

Monday, January 7, 2002

David is trying to make some arrangements over the telephone. He calls the doctor's office back in Michigan. He also calls Fort Richardson Military Reservation down in Anchorage. He has been away from his service in the Reserves since the start of this trip and he wants to get established up here. Both calls are inconclusive. He will need to do more follow up.

It is snowing. The snowfall is rather heavy. It is not so heavy that David cannot work teams however. He works several small ones nearby as usual.

As he is hooking up one of the teams, he selects Gateway and puts them into his usual wheel position. When he is returning with another dog, the last one to hook up before they go, Gateway is jumping up and down and turns toward his companion. David swiftly secures the dog in his hand. Then he turns to Gateway and the scruffing, shaking and scolding make it again obvious what he has done. This time he swiftly walks Gateway back to his own chain in the dog yard. As usual, Betty is down there too. She gives David a hand selecting a replacement wheel dog and sees them all off down the trail.

As they take off, the rest of the dog yard is in full cry jumping up and down and pleading the usual "Pick me! Pick me!" All of them except Gateway. He is lying curled up in a tight ball with his back to the departing team. He is at the end of his chain as far away from the the departing end of the yard as possible. His demeanor is somehow a mixture of misery and being angry with himself. I can't explain to you exactly how I know this but it is so. The poor guy doesn't even look up when Betty is in his area cleaning. She doesn't say anything to him. I am sure that if I can read him from here, she certainly understands what's going on from right next to him. She lets him think about what he's done.

Later David and Betty bring more doghouse pieces over from the other cabin. They begin some repairs on them. They fire up the sauna and let it begin to heat.

Nanook is moved up close to the cabin. She and her big box are in the south lean to. She seems to like being closer to people, especially her people. Brook is moved over to Nanook's former place. That way she has a longer chain and a wooden doghouse. It looks as though she likes that as she snuggles right in.

It is still snowing pretty good. Everybody has colds. We all take long relaxing saunas. They don't cure anything but I think we all feel a lot better after them.

Tuesday, January 8, 2002

The young man that was supposed to come over today, the dogsledding apprentice, never showed up. We have waited most of the day. He and David were going to go out to the truck on his snow machine. David had been planning in his head the things that the two of them could get accomplished. He has been trying to call him with the cell phone many times.

154

No answer. Cut off from everything as we are, I think we all look forward to not only help, but also contact from outsiders, probably more than we should. I think that we were making plans in our heads and looking forward to them, before we even find out if we can confirm them. Today is sort of messed up because we pretty much planned it around the young fellow coming over. Disappointing and maybe a little foolish on our part. The important thing is to make some sort of arrangement for getting out of the cabin and into town tomorrow. David spends a lot of time on the phone trying to hire someone with a snow machine. No luck!

So the day won't be a complete waste, David decides to take some small teams out on some short runs. He has the sled out and set to go. He brings up a pair of lead dogs in training and hooks them up. Then he hooks big sweet Nikolai in wheel position. And then, by golly! The die hard decides to give Gateway another chance. I watch as he walks him through the dog yard to the sled. He hooks him in place. He takes Gateway's head in his hands and lifts his face up toward his own. He is speaking to him. Then he strides swiftly to runners and jerks out the snow hook. Down the trail they go as if they are shot from guns. I watch until they are out of sight behind the trees. At that point they were still running. A while later the whole team returns... as a whole team!! It looks as though Gateway has finally learned an important lesson.

Later David tells me that he did everything he could to stack the deck in Gateway's favor. Nikolai is one of the steadiest, calmest dogs that they have. He is also totally non aggressive. By hooking Gateway next to him and by making him be the last one, he hoped that Gate wouldn't have time to be too foolish. (He doesn't mention their little 'talk'.) It certainly seems to have worked! And when Gateway returned with the team, he was fairly dancing with joy! He was so pleased with himself that he just wagged and bounced all the way back to his place in the dog yard.

I was really happy that I was here to see the successful results of that particular training technique. I was also just really happy for Gateway!

We have been discussing alternatives. If we cannot get somebody with a snow machine to give us a lift to the truck, we will need to manage on our own. Sure, it is convenient and much speedier to hire a snow machine. It is pretty expensive though. It is also an uncomfortable position to be in, to be dependent on the convenience of somebody else. It makes a person, or a group of people, feel awfully vulnerable.

OK then, for an independent alternative, dogsledders should certainly be able to get through the snow on their own. Three out of four of us have been dogsledding for years. I certainly don't put myself in the same category as David and Betty, but I have stood the runners behind a few teams in the past 40 years. Doug can ride in the basket of one of the big sleds.

We make our plans for the morning. Tomorrow night... Anchorage!

Wednesday, January 9, 2002

We are up before dawn. That is certainly not hard because the sun doesn't come up until after ten a m. David and Betty feed the dogs early. I make sure everybody gets breakfast. Then I slap together a few sandwiches for on the trail. I've had my own belongings packed for long time. We have to wait until it is light enough to get on the trail. We don't want to run into snow machines or any other hazards in the dark. David is very concerned about my feet. He rigs up something with plenty of nylon insulation and lots of laces to keep me warm for the trip out.

When it gets sort of gray outside David and Betty start to harness dogs. I take the video camera for some footage of the dog teams. Once again I take that long walk on the winding driveway. This time I am going uphill. When I get to the top, I am on a section of trail. In the summertime this is the roadway. Now it is passable only by snow machine or dog sled. I walk about 100 yards away from the driveway. There I look around and wait for the teams to come and pick me up. I final-

156

ly hear them coming up the trail. I turn on the camera and they are upon me almost before I have a chance to film. I get one fairly good shot and then the camera goes back into the bag for the trip. We have a last minute change of plan. Doug is going to stay at the cabin. Betty will stay with him too. That is disappointing all around. We don't have time to stay and discuss it very long. So pretty quickly David and I are off down the trail.

We are using the old sled with which David has won the US freight race championship many times. We skim briskly over the snow. We are running up and down some pretty substantial hills but the dogs are running with more speed and power than most dogteams do over flat trails. This is the first time I have ever actually driven any of the Britz's team. I have believed in this team and its ability from the start. I have never doubted David's or Betty's ability to know and judge objectively their capability to complete this huge challenge. But now as I stand the runners behind just a fragment of the team in training I suddenly feel with every fiber of my being, just how powerful and glorious they really are. There is not the slightest doubt in my mind that this is the team that can definitely carry David to the finish line!

As we travel I am very impressed by the lead team. They are twelve year old Wrangell and his young granddaughter, Coleen. They are incredibly responsive to any verbal commands. Even some rather strange ones like," Gee over, just a little bit." and "pay attention now." Sometimes the trail is very clear. Other times we just sort of guess where it is. The dogs seem to be doing a pretty good job of feeling it even when we really can't tell where it is. The moguls in the trail are certainly making themselves known. They are unavoidable if one is to stay on the trail. Riding up the side of the small sharp obstacle is bad enough. Thumping down off of it is worse. It is hard on the sled and the dogs don't like it. Each one jars them. It is a little similar to trying to water ski while cutting across a boat wake. Except that is very unyielding. The more we do it the less the dogs like it. The only thing we can really do for them is to verbally encourage them. They are very responsive to this.

Soon we have joined the main trail and are running as smoothly as we can over those annoying lumps. For some reason I look back over my shoulder. The rising sun strikes and illuminates a white peak. At first I think it is the only mountain around. Then I realize that it is surrounded by a whole range. It stands out "head and shoulders" above the rest. I call David's attention to it. He tells me it is Denali. It is also about 25 miles away. It looks like it is right behind us. As if I could step off the sled and walk back to it in about ten minutes. It is impressive. This is the first time I have seen Denali.

Then I realize I am seeing Denali for the first time in my life while standing on the runners behind, what I am sure are some of the best Alaskan malamutes in the world. My first trip to Alaska and I am actually dogsledding a team of this quality through the edge of the Alaska range. If I die right this minute, I die happy! I don't even need to worry about going to Heaven... I'm there.

The feeling of elation is wonderful! On the practical side however, no matter how happy I am, I'd really just as soon not die right now. So I had better pay attention to what I am doing. The remainder of the run, just a few more good hills to the parking lot, will always remain in my heart and my spirit.

We round a curve and start down the last hill. A sheer wall of rock and ice rises vertically to my left. To my right is the gorge that I had noticed so long ago from the seat of the rental truck. The trail zigs and zags a little as it drops sharply to the bridge across that gorge. In my brain I know that the trail is wide enough for a pickup truck to navigate. My acrophobia is telling me different. I have no time to think about fear. The thrill and exhilaration override it. Keep your two bit phony roller coasters of civilization. This is real!!

We make the bridge and then the turn, and then run uphill to the parking lot. I remember stopping, jumping off the runners to hold the dogs, and then snapping them on chains around the truck. To be honest, I don't even know if I helped

David beyond that or not. I do remember later helping to locate supplies in the rental truck and putting them out for David to take back to the cabin on his return trip.

As David maneuvers the four wheel drive truck up the hill on the other side of the parking lot, it's suddenly like no big deal now. We are heading back to what I know as the real world. As anxious as I am to get back to mine... I suddenly hate to leave.

Daddy

Hugs

Boost!!

Since I Left - Epilogue

Now that I am in the lower 48 I am trying my best to keep in touch. The cell phone is better than nothing, but not much. It needs frequent recharging so energy for it is conserved as much as possible. We have an arrangement for them to turn it on at certain times once or twice a week. Then we are at the mercy of the elements. Their location in the Matanuska Valley (Yup! Betty's a Valley girl) is not the best area for a telephone signal to penetrate, either incoming or outgoing. Most of the time the static overwhelms conversation so badly we have to hang up before too long. Sometimes we get cut in on or we cut in and out of other people's conversations. But that and the U.S. Postal Service are about all we have for now.

Before I left Betty and David had both been giving Q.T. some extra attention. She was not running with the team well at all. They tried running her with just Greyling beside her. She would do that alright but still didn't seem happy with a bigger team. Betty also noticed that she was the one female that was not popping in and out of heat. In fact, she hadn't been in heat since well before leaving Michigan. (I am perpetually amazed by Betty's command of the millions of details she keeps on track.) So Betty put her on an herbal remedy to help maintain "female health". Soon she came into a very strong heat. Her body seemed to be casting out some nasty stuff. She acted like she didn't feel well for a couple of days and then she perked right up. Since then she has been running with the team happily !

The Dream Team have moved from Norman Vaughan's dog handler's cabin to a cabin belonging to Martin Buser. The first cabin was so very remote that it was a major undertaking every time they wanted to go into town. Besides if those darn moguls are tough enough to rip the bolts out of a truck they also proved tough enough to ruin dogsleds. David has built 3 only to have them pounded to pieces on the trail. It is not as if David doesn't know how to build dogsleds. He has been building them for years. In fact, he built the ones he won the freight races with. David was getting pretty tired of building and rebuilding sleds when Martin Buser acknowledged that the moguls around there are too rough on equipment and offered to rent them his spare cabin, at least for awhile. There

is no electricity there, of course. In fact, the pump doesn't work so water for everything and everybody must be melted from snow or carried from the river. But it is close enough to the big parking lot that they can drive the 4-wheel drive dog truck in to it. Martin even had the long driveway plowed out. It made the outside world once again within reach. You bet they moved!

Since then, spring has come to Alaska. When they come back I know we will be getting plenty of tales about the wet Alaskan springtime.

As of this writing they are seeking another place. Preferably one they can stay in for the rest of their time up there. Martin Buser needs his place back so he can get some training going soon. August is the start of the season.

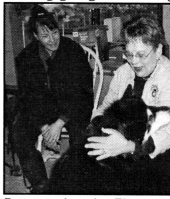

Betty introduces her Elim to Joan Jackson. JJ is the author of Elim: The Determined Athlete

One day when David was running the team, he saw a moose off to one side of the trail. He tried to keep the team over to the other side of the trail. He hoped to slip past it unnoticed. That might have worked too if Gateway had not decided that he was interested in the moose, or its droppings. (Some dogs very attracted to moose droppings.) He pulled the team over in that direction. It turned, saw them, and charged. David was trying to drive the team away to safety when the sled hit a mogul just the wrong way and overturned. He couldn't even get at the shotgun in the sled bag. About that time the moose decided that David looked as though he would make a pretty good target. It turned from the team and started toward him. Suddenly Elim was between the

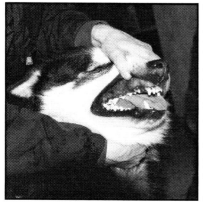

two of them! He was barking and snarling. The moose kicked Elim in the face, the body and anywhere else it could. Elim was busy snarling and biting the moose in the legs which were the only part of it he could reach easily. That was too much. The moose ran away.

When they got back home Elim was very obviously sore. He did not want to be touched. Especially around his poor face. After a brief recuperation time he did allow them to go over him thoroughly. When they checked his face and his mouth, they discovered that he was missing one fang.

A few weeks after that incident, Elim was healed up and feeling well enough to run with the team again. David had him hooked into a 10-dog team. They had just left the cabin and headed down the trail. Suddenly they came upon a moose and her calf. The baby ran away but the mother turned and ran right into the team. Again David tried to maintain control of the team and drive them away from her. With all the chaos of the moose and dogs and those dog-gone moguls in the trail, the sled flipped over again. This time David was struck in the face and thrown down. This incident cost David a tooth.

David displays the tooth he chipped in his encounter with the moose. Even with the yellow lenses, you can see the twinkle in his eyes.

Betty was still at the cabin when she heard all the commotion. She knew that David had just started down the trail and thought he might have a tangle or some other problem. Even with their dogs, there is always the possibility a fight can happen. She went out of the cabin and started down the trail toward the sound of the ruckus. As she approached that area she saw something large and dark coming at her fast!

The moose had struck and pounded its way through the team and run past it and David. Alaska had slipped out of his harness (or was knocked out of it.) and run to the dog truck. It was something with which he was familiar. It was probably what he thought of as a place of safety. As Betty realized that it was rushing at her, she stepped off of the trail to let it go by. It probably would have run right past her but it suddenly became aware of the dog yard full of the rest of the malamutes at the end of the pathway. She (the moose) started to turn to run past the truck to get away. Alaska was standing there. The look of deep concern on his face (and probably more than a little fear) must have looked, threatening to her. Behind her, the team was running for home in a tangle with the sled bouncing along more beside them than behind them. The moose turned the only way that seemed to be open. There stood Betty.

One slim human woman certainly must have seemed the least fearsome of all the options. Two pairs of brown eyes met...all in fear. Even with their eyes locked together, Betty was very aware of those powerful, dinner-plate-sized hooves! The moose started toward Betty but then hesitated. Between them had appeared a large dark wolfish form. Elim had very recently received a very tough lesson on the speed and power in the legs and hooves of a moose. Yet he chose to face this one rather than to allow his precious Betty to suffer such a fate!

Barking, snarling and growling, he did his best to give as good as he got. Things could have gone even worse when suddenly there were two dark wolfish forms between Betty and the moose. Elim's best friend and look-alike brother, Nikolai, had joined the fray! Whether the moose thought she was seeing double or just could not cope with being outnumbered, no one knows — or cares. She turned and leaped past the team (which was now close also). She ran off up the trail. David managed to avoid her as she bolted past him and disappeared into the wilderness.

There was blood all over the snow. Betty and David brought Elim into the cabin. A later inspection would show him to be bruised underneath his fur, from his face to his hips. But right then the immediate concern was his bleeding. Poor Elim's face had a deep cut under the eye. It was bleeding profusely. An artery had been ruptured. They tried to phone to get a vet to respond.... no luck! They were already performing direct pressure first aid. Betty resorted to her good old herbal remedy. They applied a cayenne pepper tincture that was supposed to control bleeding. It worked! Elim was saved!

He had to stay in the cabin for awhile to rest and recuperate. He liked that. He was still in the middle of his healing time in March, so he was not allowed to participate in running a 200 + mile training race with most of the rest of his team. Since then, however, he has made a full recovery. He is anxious to begin fall training with everybody else. His spirit remains undaunted.

The Dream Team continues...
The Dream goes on !

The End!

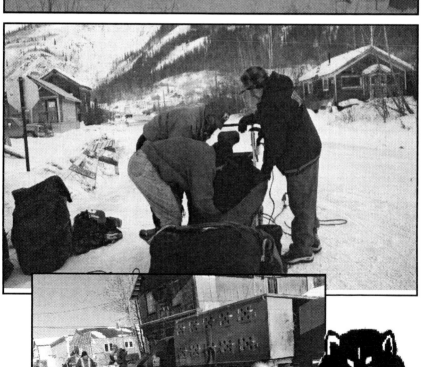